Gender Diversity, Recognition and Citizenship

Citizenship, Gender and Diversity

Series Editors: **Beatrice Halsaa**, University of Oslo, Norway; **Sasha Roseneil**, Birkbeck College, University of London, UK; and **Sevil Sumer**, University of Bergen, Norway

Titles include:

Beatrice Halsaa, Sasha Roseneil, and Sevil Sumer (*editors*)
REMAKING CITIZENSHIP IN MULTICULTURAL EUROPE
Women's Movements, Gender and Diversity

Sally Hines
GENDER DIVERSITY, RECOGNITION AND CITIZENSHIP
Towards a Politics of Difference

Line Nyhagen Predelli, Beatrice Halsaa, Cecile Thun, and Adriana Sandu (*editors*)
MAJORITY–MINORITY RELATIONS IN CONTEMPORARY WOMEN'S MOVEMENTS
Strategic Sisterhood

Sasha Roseneil
BEYOND CITIZENSHIP?
Feminism and the Transformation of Belonging

Ana Cristina Santos
SOCIAL MOVEMENTS AND SEXUAL CITIZENSHIP IN SOUTHERN EUROPE

Citizenship, Gender and Diversity
Series Standing Order ISBN 978–0–23028054–0 Hardback
978–0–23028055–7 Paperback
(*outside North America only*)

You can receive future titles in this series as they are published by placing a standing order. Please contact your bookseller or, in case of difficulty, write to us at the address below with your name and address, the title of the series and the ISBN quoted above.

Customer Services Department, Macmillan Distribution Ltd, Houndmills, Basingstoke, Hampshire RG21 6XS, England

Gender Diversity, Recognition and Citizenship

Towards a Politics of Difference

Sally Hines
University of Leeds, UK

palgrave
macmillan

First published 2013 by
PALGRAVE MACMILLAN

Palgrave Macmillan in the UK is an imprint of Macmillan Publishers Limited, registered in England, company number 785998, of Houndmills, Basingstoke, Hampshire RG21 6XS.

Palgrave Macmillan in the US is a division of St Martin's Press LLC, 175 Fifth Avenue, New York, NY 10010.

Palgrave Macmillan is the global academic imprint of the above companies and has companies and representatives throughout the world.

Palgrave® and Macmillan® are registered trademarks in the United States, the United Kingdom, Europe and other countries.

ISBN 978–0–230–27189–0

This book is printed on paper suitable for recycling and made from fully managed and sustained forest sources. Logging, pulping and manufacturing processes are expected to conform to the environmental regulations of the country of origin.

A catalogue record for this book is available from the British Library.

A catalog record for this book is available from the Library of Congress.

For Margaret Hines

'The denial of the right to be different is the denial of right to be'.

Gilles Deleuze, *Difference and Repetition*

'You're equal but different
It's obvious
So obvious'

The Au Pairs, *It's Obvious*

Contents

Acknowledgements

I am grateful to the Economic and Social Research Council for funding the two projects that motivated this book: first, 'Gender Diversity, Recognition and Citizenship' (2008–2010: RES-000-22-2763) and, second, 'Recognising Diversity? Equalities in Principle and Practice' (2012–2013: ES/J010960/1). I would like to thank Zowie Davy for her wonderful work as research assistant on the first project. Zowie carried out all the interviews upon which this book draws, and their richness is due to her interviewing skills – she is also the queen of NVivo! Thanks to Diane Richardson and Surya Monro for their input into this research as members of the advisory board. Many thanks to Stefanie Boulila for her great work as project assistant on the second project.

I am very grateful to the people who participated in both research projects: in individual interviews, focus groups, workshops and seminars. I owe much gratitude to members of transgender organisations and campaigning groups who supported the second project, and especially to James Morton from 'Scottish Transgender Alliance'; Alice Purnell, from GENDYS; Bernard and Terry Reed from GIRES; and Christie Elan Cane, who endorsed the proposal.

I would also like to thank Philippa Grand and Naomi Robinson at Palgrave Macmillan, Devasena Vedamurthi at Integra Software Services and the Series Editors of *Citizenship, Gender and Diversity* for their support of this book project. Some parts of chapters in this book have appeared in different forms in previous works. Sections of Chapter 2 have appeared in an earlier form in the chapter 'Riding the Waves: Feminism, Lesbian and Gay Politics, and the Transgender Debates' in Gurminder Bhambra and Ipek Demir's edited book, *1968 in Retrospect: History, Politics, Alterity* (2009: Palgrave Macmillan). Sections of Chapter 3 have appeared in an earlier form in the journal article 'A Pathway to Diversity?: Human Rights, Citizenship and Politics of Transgender' in the special human rights issue of the journal *Contemporary Politics* (15: 1) edited by Matthew Waites and

Kelly Kolman, which was then developed into the edited book *The Global Politics of LGBT Human Rights* (2010: Routledge). Sections of Chapter 5 have appeared in an earlier form in the chapter 'Stirring It Up-Again: A Politics of Difference in the New Millennium' in the book *Sexualities: Past Reflections, Future Directions* (2012: Palgrave Macmillan) that Yvette Taylor and I edited. Sections of Chapter 4 have appeared in an earlier form in 'Recognising Diversity? Transgender Citizenship and the Gender Recognition Act' in the book *Transgender Identities: Towards a Social Analysis of Gender Diversity* (2012: Routledge) that Tam Sanger and I edited.

Many thanks to friends and colleagues (including MA and PhD students) in the Centre for Interdisciplinary Gender Studies and the School of Sociology and Social Policy at the University of Leeds. There is a vibrant community of academics and activists in the areas of gender, sexuality and transgender studies whose work inspires mine. I am deeply indebted to these networks of people – many of whom I draw on in this book. Many of these people are also great colleagues and friends – big thanks to you all for making work such fun! Thanks also to Fiona Williams, Sasha Roseneil, Diane Richardson, Jeffrey Weeks and Judith Halberstam who continue to offer generous support in a number of ways to my work. I owe special thanks to a group of people who are both close working partners and close friends: Surya Monro, Zowie Davy, Yvette Taylor, and Tam Sanger. May the collaborations and the good times continue. Thanks to my wider networks of friends for fun, frolics and friendship, and a special mention here to Su Brown for everything oldest-matey!

Finally, deepest thanks to my family whose love, care and support in so many ways is ever present in my life; to Margaret Hines, Barry Hines, Gil Jackson-Hines, Mark Jackson, Jean Pension, Tom Hines, Helen Owen and Eve Hines; to Richard Hines, Jackie Hines, Tim Jackson and Jo Stancliife. This book is dedicated to my mum, Margaret Hines, who supports me in every possible way and who proof read every word, comma and colon of this manuscript (still, any errors are entirely mine!).

Introduction

'Transgender' has emerged as a subject of growing social, cultural and social-scientific interest in recent years. Alongside an ever-increasing cultural focus on transgender, for example, in the media and popular culture, shifting attitudes towards transgender people are evident through recent legislative changes across many countries in Europe, and in the UK by the Gender Recognition Act (GRA, 2004). These social, cultural and legislative developments reflect the ways in which gender diversity is acquiring visibility in contemporary society and mark transgender as an important and timely area of study.

There is a growing body of scholarship, which falls within the area of transgender studies that examines the formation of transgender identities (Ekins and King, 1996; Ekins, 1997; Prosser, 1998; Davy, 2010). While very important, this work is largely focused upon the formation of transgender identities through and/or in opposition to medical discourse and practice. There is a psychological literature that has looked at the sexuality of trans people (Clare, 1984; Bockting and Coleman, 1992). However, this work concentrates upon sexuality within an individualised context by focusing upon sexual self-identities of transgender people. There is a body of sociological literature in the United States that examines transgender identities and sexual relationships (Devor, 1987, 1989; Lewins, 1995; Cromwell, 1999), though there is little work in this area within a British context – that of Tam Sanger (2010) being an exception. Some British work has broadly examined transgender political movements (Monro, 2005; Ekins and King, 2006; Stryker and Whittle, 2006); however, this work predates the Gender Recognition Act (GRA, 2004).

The impact of recent legislation upon transgender identities and practices of intimacy, then, remains underexplored. This book seeks to fill this gap, while contributing to the literature outlined above, by examining the impact of recent UK legislation – the UK Gender Recognition Act (2004) – on the social construction of transgender identity practices, and upon individual and collective experiences of transgender. Representing the civil recognition of gender transition, the GRA marks an important change in attitudes towards transgender people, enabling the change of birth certificates and granting transgender people the right to marry in their acquired gender. Crucially, the legislation detaches the legal recognition of 'sex' from the requirement of surgical intervention, and thus brings a new framework for understanding 'sex' and gender, and the relationship between these concepts. Moreover, the GRA addresses employment and welfare issues through its clause that transgender people who successfully register under the GRA for a Gender Recognition Certificate (GRC) will no longer be required to disclose their former gender identity status to professional bodies. Transgender is thus an arena in which questions of gendered, sexual, intimate and embodied identity and citizenship are being debated, contested and reconfigured. Drawing on an empirical study of the impact of the UK Gender Recognition Act (GRA, 2004) upon practices of gender and sexual diversity, the book examines the GRA through a number of social, cultural, legal and policy contexts, and in relation to a range of academic, political, legal and policy debates.

Struggles for the 'recognition of difference' have long been central to emancipatory politics of gender, sexuality, race and ethnicity, and claims for the recognition of difference now drive many social and political conflicts (Fraser, 2000). Subsequently, the concept of 'recognition' has been the subject of much recent debate within social and political theory (Young, 1990; Fraser, 1995; Honneth, 1995; Taylor, 1995; Butler, 1998; McNay, 2008). This book seeks to contribute to theoretical debates around recognition and also to empirically consider the meanings, significance and experience of recognition in relation to the Gender Recognition Act. To these ends, Chapter 1 considers the role of 'recognition' within social movements and political theory and looks in detail at the work of key figures in the recognition literature. Chapter 2 follows by taking a more substantive approach to claims for recognition based on gender, sexuality and, later, transgender since the 1960s. Central to Chapter 2 is the exploration of issues of connection and disconnection across and between different social movements around gender and sexuality as they moved to claim recognition.

Claims for recognition are central to human rights discourse and law. Moreover, 'recognition' has been at the heart of claims to equality that, over the last decade, have been brought under the Human Rights Act (HRA). A number of these claims have been brought by trans people who have argued that the UK government failed to protect their rights to equality. Chapter 3 examines these key moments leading to legal change in detail. It also considers the ways in which a universal language of rights is, to great detriment, a cornerstone of human rights based law.

Chapter 4 then turns to empirical research findings to explore the significance of the UK Gender Recognition Act (GRA, 2004) for research participants as it came into law. The title of Chapter 4 'Claiming and Contesting Recognition' speaks of the ways in which the chapter critically evaluates the significance of recognition, taking account of the reasons why participants chose not to register, as well as why others did. In a similar vein, Chapter 5 explores the impact of the GRA on intimate and sexual diversities. Here a range of literature on intimate, sexual and personal life is examined in relation to participants' narratives.

In Chapter 6, the emergence of transgender rights is explored within the context of UK New Labour Government's focus on equality and diversity. The materialisation of human rights discourse and law maps on to a post-1997 policy focus on equalities and diversity to which issues of gender and sexuality have been central. The chapter examines the UK Gender Recognition Act (GRA, 2004) in relation to a number of equality and diversity laws, policies and broader initiatives that have been at the forefront of the policy agendas of the last two UK governments. Moreover, the GRA will be considered alongside other legal developments, which address issues of gender and sexual equality. A key question for this chapter is the governance of diversity. In exploring this issue, the chapter draws on debates around sexual and gendered citizenship and reflects on recent studies that have examined the implementation of equality and diversity. In this chapter, I also present a critique of recognition theory and politics in relation to its demands for assimilation and 'sameness'. This argument is taken further in the final chapter of the book.

Chapter 7 speaks back to changing notions and experiences of gendered and sexual citizenship and examines issues of inclusion/exclusion in relation to a range of gendered and sexual identity positions and intimate practices that have been considered in preceding chapters. In turn, issues of inclusion/exclusion lead back to questions of 'difference'. Accordingly, the final chapter of the book considers whether transgender narratives on the impact and significance of the GRA speak more fully to a 'politics of difference' (Young, 1990) than to politics of recognition, rights or citizenship. In Chapter 7 I thus develop my critique of recognition theory and politics and argue that Iris Marion Young's (1990) thesis of a 'politics of difference' provides a stronger set of theoretical *and* political tools for accounting for gender and sexual diversity. This latter point is echoed in the Conclusion of the book, as I reflect on possibilities of 'doing' diversity through knowledge sharing across academic and non-academic communities.

As a whole, the book considers recent legislative and policy changes within the context of an increasing cultural and social focus on gender diversity. Further, it examines how gender recognition speaks to other recent policy shifts around gender and sexuality and to current theoretical debates around the concepts of recognition, human rights and citizenship. In drawing on empirical and substantive material, alongside theoretical debate, the book seeks to throw new light on the individual and collective experiences of transgender people within the context of broader social, legal, and policy changes around gender and sexuality. The book also aims to address the social relations, identities and cultural values that shape changing law and policy and to examine the ways in which 'experience' is constructed through these in turn. While the focus of the book is on UK law and policy and draws on empirical material collected in the United Kingdom, similar debates and changes are occurring across Europe at social, cultural, political, policy and legal levels.

The project

This book draws on original empirical material that was collected for a project titled 'Gender Diversity, Recognition and Citizenship'. The project was funded by the UK Economic and Social Research Council (ESRC) and took place between May 2008 and May 2010. The project sought to address the impacts and the significance of the GRA by considering how transgender people variously understand and experience this changing policy landscape. Research questions asked were as follows:

1. Why some people view the GRA as significant and register for 'gender recognition', and why others do not.
2. How married people are negotiating the choice between gender recognition and the recognition of their partnerships.
3. The extent to which gender recognition characterises continuities and/or changes to the medicalisation of transgender.
4. To what extent the GRA moves beyond a binary gender model.

Various qualitative methods were employed to collect data, including textual/policy analysis, 25 in-depth one-to-one interviews, 2 focus groups with 8 and 9 members each, one-to-one interviews and analysis of virtual materials – for example, online blogs, chat rooms and discussion forums. Interview and focus group participants were recruited through transgender support groups, self-help groups and campaigning groups. Some participants were introduced to us through existing participants or word of mouth. Sampling strategies aimed to maximise diversity, while recognising that a study of this size cannot claim to be representative. To these ends, sampling criteria for the individual interview participants consisted of the following:

Gender: 18 participants defined themselves as women or female; 5 participants defined themselves as male or FtM (female to male); 1 participant described themself as non-gendered; 1 participant defined as gender queer.

Sexuality: 8 participants identified as heterosexual; 4 participants identified as bisexual; 4 participants identified as lesbian; 1 participant identified as gay; 2 participants identified as queer; 1 participant identified as pansexual; 1 participant identified as asexual; 2 participants said that it was 'difficult to say' what their sexuality was; 2 participants were reluctant to talk about their sexuality.

Age: 2 participants were aged 20–30 yrs; 4 participants were aged 30–40 yrs; 5 participants were aged 40–50 yrs; 8 participants were aged 50–60 yrs; 5 participants were aged 60+; 1 participant did not want to reveal their age.

Relationship status: 14 participants were in relationships and/or married/civilly partnered: of these, 6 participants were in relationships with their pre-transition partners and two were in civil partnerships; 11 participants were single.
Parenting status: 9 participants had children.

Participants were also from a range of occupational groups, including professionals, self-employed, skilled and unskilled, temporary workers, students and unemployed. The majority of participants were from urban areas, although seven were from small towns or villages. All participants resided in the United Kingdom. A major weakness in the sampling strategy, and thus of the research as a whole, is that the vast majority of participants were white British. Despite purposive sampling, only two of those interviewed were identified as non-British and only one was from a minority ethnic background.

Twelve participants had successfully applied for a GRC. One participant had applied and received an Interim Certificate; three participants had unsuccessfully applied for a GRC; six participants were unable to apply for a GRC due to not meeting the application criteria; three participants had chosen not to apply for a GRC even though they met the criteria for application.

Representing the civil recognition of gender transition, the UK Gender Recognition Act (GRA, 2004) marks an important change in attitudes towards trans people, enabling the change of birth certificates and granting trans people the right to marry in their acquired gender. These developments reflect broader social changes around the conceptualisation and the practices of identity and illustrate how questions of gendered, sexual, intimate and embodied identity and citizenship are being debated, contested and reconfigured in contemporary society. While examining central academic, legal and policy debates, subsequent chapters of the book also explore the understandings and experiences of some of the people who are living through these changes – their stories are at the heart of the book.

1
Theorising Recognition

Introduction

This chapter is structured into two sections. The first section begins by considering the role of 'recognition' within social movement and political theory. Since the 1960s, the notion of recognition has been central to social movement struggles for equality across the arenas of social class, race, embodiment, gender and sexuality, and related issues of identity are the drivers of recognition claims. At the same time, recent social and political theory has examined the meaning and significance of 'recognition'. In this way, scholars have set out differing parameters when considering the relevance of recognition for social justice. This chapter begins, then, by thinking about the academic turn to recognition alongside the fracturing of social democratic ideals, and especially the rise of identity politics and new social movements, in the late 1960s.

The second part of this section hones in on conceptualisations of recognition in considering the work of key figures in the literature. First, I look in detail at the approaches of Axel Honneth (1995), Charles Taylor (1995) and Nancy Fraser (1995). The chapter then turns to the redistribution/recognition debate. Here Fraser's work is considered alongside that of Iris Marion Young (1997), Judith Butler (1998) and, again, Axel Honneth. Reading deliberations of redistribution/recognition allows further consideration of the correlation of political theories of recognition and cultural politics of identity. These themes are elaborated as the chapter examines work that has directly addressed gender and sexuality through recognition theory.

The second section of the chapter turns to the UK GRA. First, I outline the clause and criteria of the GRA to assess arguments surrounding redistribution/recognition in the literature previously discussed. Second, I empirically consider understandings of the concept of 'recognition' as it is configured in the aptly named Gender *Recognition* Act (UK, 2004). While subsequent chapters empirically examine the significance and the experiences of the Act as it came into law, here I reflect on how research participants conceptualised the term 'recognition' itself. The ways in which participants understood recognition are important for later considerations of how the GRA came to be experienced and, particularly, for exploring the ways in which participants view the Act as having different degrees of significance. The chapter closes by considering the extent to which academic debates around recognition resonate or conflict with the understandings of research participants.

Recognising recognition

The notion of 'recognition' forms the backdrop to varied political claims – some distinct and others overlapping – concerning identity, citizenship, material distribution and restoration, which, in turn, speak to national and global structural patterns of (in)equality and routes to social justice. Claims for recognition formulate through a number of identity sites including those related to class, race, ethnicity, nation, religion, the body (for example, around politics of disability), sexuality and gender, and are strongly contested – both institutionally and by other recognition seekers. Politics of recognition in the West emerged from the fracturing of social democratic ideals in the late 1960s, whereby political identification became less tied to social class and occupation. As Simon Thompson remarks, 'Into this vacated space, so-called new social movements have emerged to present a novel sort of challenge to the politics of social democracy' (2006: 2). Similarly, Steven Seidman (1997) links the development of recognition claims to an emergent politics of identity in the 1960s. Claims for recognition became articulated on the basis of race, ethnicity and nationhood through the Civil Rights Movement and struggles for multiculturalism; gender through the Women's Movement; embodiment through the Disability Rights Movement; and sexuality through Sexual Liberation.

While the *principles* of recognition politics – respect, resources, protection, rights and benefits – have a long and global history, *discourses* of recognition – the ways in which these principles were articulated – shifted. Rather than claims for equality based upon *sameness*, social movements in the 1960s developed a language of *difference*. This marked an emerging self-consciousness and self-confidence among social movements (Seidman, 1997), or, as McLaughlin, Phillimore and Richardson suggest, a politics of reflexivity: 'What changed was the naming of these dynamics, the political reflexivity which came to recognise recognition itself as salient [...]' (2011: 2). The principle of 'difference' thus became central to standards of social justice. Concurrently, a politics of retribution – whereby historical wrongs and practices of injustice (for example, slavery in the United States; the Holocaust in Germany; apartheid in South Africa) were institutionally recognised and expressed – globally took shape (Phillips, 2003). Indeed, issues of race, ethnicity and national belonging and becoming were central to early reflections on the importance of recognition to postcolonial theory (Fanon, 1952), and later considerations of diaspora (Hall, 1990). At conceptual and political levels, then, 'recognising recognition' (McLaughlin et al., 2011: 2) incurred longitudinal reflexivity – looking back to social injustices of the past to acknowledge harms committed, to consider their impact in the present and to forge justice for the future. These themes, and especially the question of routes to social justice, are central to recognition debates and are assessed differently by each of the writers considered below.

Debating recognition: Honneth, Taylor and Fraser

Each of the writers considered here have overlapping concerns; each is concerned with theorising means by which to bring about social justice. Each also links the emergence of recognition to claims of new social movements as discussed above. For Axel Honneth (1995), recognition politics can be characterised by a shared sense of becoming – a collective identity. Charles Taylor argues that contemporary politics 'turn on the need, sometimes the demand for recognition [...] on behalf of minority or "subaltern" groups, in some forms of feminism, and in what is called the politics of multiculturalism' (1995: 225). Following Habermas (1994), both Honneth and Taylor suggest that the need for recognition is pre-rational; humans are driven not by self-interest but by the desire for understanding and reciprocity.

From a different premise, Nancy Fraser (1995) also underscores the notion of identity in her discussion of recognition: 'A great many contemporary social movements can only be properly understood from a normative point of view if their motivating demands are interpreted along the lines of a "politics of identity" – a demand for the cultural recognition of their collective identity' (2003: 111). Each of these writers agree that political arenas have moved beyond a previous overriding focus on social class and, moreover, on issues of material redistribution. Yet recent years have seen a return to class by writers arguing for the increased salience of class as both an identity and as a marker of growing material inequalities in capitalist societies (Skeggs, 1997; Hennessy, 2000; Savage, 2000; Taylor, 2012). It is alongside social class, then, not in the place of, that issues of identity, culture, and difference have come to the fore.

Honneth, Taylor and Fraser also concur on the significance of recognition, each engaging with recognition not only as means by which to understand the contemporary political terrain, but as a method of achieving social justice. As Thompson discusses, each writer 'articulates a political theory of recognition which is based on the premise that a just society would be one in which everyone gets due recognition. In such a society, in other words, all individuals and groups would enjoy the practical acknowledgment that they deserve' (2006: 3). Later chapters of this book will indicate that recognition claims, however, are far from democratic. Rather, demands for collective recognition are frequently pitted against those of other groups. For now, though, my point is to trace connecting themes in the work of Honneth, Taylor and Fraser. In this way, each writer suggests that recognition lies at the heart of social justice. Honneth (1995) argues that, since the development of the self is a dialogical process, recognition is key to social inclusion. Liberal states should strive to enable both social recognition and autonomy. This balance, he believes, prevents 'anti-social striving for independence' (2002: 504). Honneth goes so far as to map human development in terms of recognition, or, at least, to suggest that recognition struggles emerge from elemental desire to avoid the 'moral suffering' that arises from 'misrecognition'.

Taylor (1995) also suggests that social justice depends on recognition and proposes that collective recognition be included into politics of rights. For Taylor, then, recognition of the self – or self-identity – is dependent on the recognition of others. The alternative, he argues, is to invite 'nonrecognition' or 'misrecognition', which 'can inflict harm, can be a form of oppression, imprisoning someone in a false, distorted, reduced mode of being' (1995: 25). Later chapters of this book return to Taylor's notions of non-recognition and misrecognition, arguing for the significance of these terms when considering recognition of gender diversity. Here, though, it is important to reflect on Taylor's intervention: misrecognition is a process of oppression. Fraser (1995) also invokes the effects of misrecognition, suggesting that when misrecognition of social status occurs, it reduces the ability to be a social actor:

> To be misrecognised is to be denied the status of a full partner in social interaction and to be prevented from participating as a peer in social life as a consequence of institutionalized patterns of cultural value that constitutes one as comparatively unworthy of respect.
>
> Fraser (2003: 27)

As Fraser links misrecognition to 'unworthiness', Honneth talks about the significance of recognition for the self to 'appear in public without shame' (2004: 355). Here, then, recognition holds important affective qualities and is fundamental to emotional characteristics – self-worth, respect and dignity. Honneth's (1995) discussion of 'struggles' around recognition thus draws attention to the impacts of social visibility and acknowledgement. 'Struggles' arise when individuals or groups feel invisible or unacknowledged, and, hence, excluded. Inclusion is therefore central to recognition as are equality and visibility. If recognition is based on equality and inclusion, however, what happens to the acknowledgement of claims by groups who do not want to be included in dominant political life and who refute notions of equality? Later chapters consider these questions in relation to gender and sexual diversity.

The significance of the affective and the emotional run through recognition debates. In his seminal essay 'The Politics of Recognition' (1992), Taylor distinguishes between the 'intimate sphere' and the 'public sphere'. On the former, he situates love (affective and intimate relationships) as central to identity and thus to recognition. On the latter, he differentiates between two aspects of public recognition: a 'politics of universalism', through which autonomy is protected in the granting of rights, and a 'politics of difference', which protects individual identity. The fissures between a politics of universalism and a politics of difference run through subsequent chapters of this book and are reflected on directly in Chapter 7. Honneth (1995) also writes of the significance of love as an affective attachment to personal identity. He adds on to this the importance of rational autonomy – or respect – to a universal model of recognition and draws attention to the recognition of esteem, which he sees as arising through collective values. The place of respect and esteem within recognition struggles will be further explored towards the end of this chapter in empirical consideration of the GRA. While Honneth, and to a lesser extent, Taylor, draws on psychoanalysis to link the emotional and the political – the self, the intimate and the public – Fraser refutes the place of psychoanalysis in political theory. Moreover, she argues strongly against developing political theory through accounts of individual subjectivity. Instead, Fraser insists that recognition and, by turn, misrecognition, is located in social and political structures. It is from this premise that Fraser foregrounds socio-economic redistribution in theorising a politics of recognition.

Material redistribution and cultural recognition

The rise of a politics of recognition has been discussed as a paradigm shift (Hobson, 2003) wherein concerns over redistribution of material resources have been overshadowed by claims for respect based on individual or group difference. Indeed, Fraser repeatedly argues that: 'we are facing a new constellation in the grammar of political claims making. In this constellation, the center of gravity has shifted "from redistribution to recognition" (Fraser, 1995)' (2003: 22). Fraser explains:

> The usual approach is to view recognition through the lens of identity. From this perspective, what requires recognition is group-specific cultural identity. Misrecognition consists in the depreciation of such identity by the dominant culture and the consequent

> damage to group members' sense of self. Redressing this harm requires engaging in a politics of recognition. In such a politics, group members join together to refashion their collective identity by producing a self-affirming culture of their own. Thus, on the identity model of recognition, the politics of recognition means 'identity politics'.
>
> Fraser (2003: 23)

From different premises, later chapters of this book, reject a model of identity politics for accounting for, and protecting, gender diversity. I argue that a politics of identity has operated as an excluding mechanism. In Chapter 7, I suggest that a politics of recognition is harboured by its ties to identity as an authentic characteristic and argue for the potentials of a politics of difference. Fraser's original point of contention with recognition politics is, however, a different one. In her essay 'From Redistribution to Recognition? Dilemma's of Justice in a "Postsocialist Age"', published in *New Left Review* in 1995, Fraser states the importance of economic redistribution in enabling social justice (Fraser, 1995). In her view, the 'identity model' has brought about 'the displacement of redistribution by recognition' (2003: 24). In other words, issues of cultural difference have become more important in contemporary politics than economic inequalities.

Fraser is not alone among political theorists in arguing that a 'cultural turn' has displaced issues of economic inequality (Phillips, 2003). Key thinkers within political theory subsequently argued that increasing material divisions in society were being ignored through an increasing focus on identity and difference. Brian Barry and Richard Rorty offer extreme examples of this position. In responding to the argument that the Left fails to take adequate account of racial difference, Barry responded that 'it is multiculturalists who are blind to the ever-widening differences that are such a deplorable feature of most contemporary societies [...] in the quality of education and healthcare available to people with different incomes' (2001: 63–64). Similarly Rorty believes that there are 'dangerous consequences of developing a left that neglects class and money by focusing on the elimination of prejudice and sexism' (2000: 18). Of course, the contention from white men on the Left that a focus on race and gender (and sexuality) dilutes attention from the class struggle is not new, and Chapter 2 maps the impacts of such argument on the emergence of social movements based around gender, sexuality and, later, gender diversity. It is important to note that Fraser herself did not fit with a Leftist position that denied the significance of identity to contemporary politics and models of social justice. Fraser's interjection was as a theorist of recognition herself and, as earlier discussion indicates, her work is deeply concerned with the harms endured through misrecognition: 'a politics of recognition is politically useful and indeed morally required' (2008: 83). Indeed Fraser offers a direct challenge to Rorty's rejection of recognition politics: 'I conclude that the Left should reject Rorty's proposal to turn back the clock. [...] it should build on the gains of the last forty years, which have expanded and deepened the meaning of social justice' (2008: 88). Hence, in contrast to Barry and Rorty, Fraser does not propose a move away from a politics of culture (recognition). Rather she argues for the need to (re)instate an economic model of social justice (redistribution) in conjunction with a politics of recognition. For Fraser, then, a model of social justice must equally concern aspects of recognition and redistribution.

Yet Fraser *does* pit social class and economic equality against identity and difference, or, at least, views them as distinct facets of social justice: 'Insofar as the politics of recognition is displacing the politics of redistribution, it risks aiding the forces that promote economic equality' (2003: 22), and, it is in this vein, that Fraser has been critiqued for reinforcing a material/cultural divide. Accordingly, Iris Marion-Young has argued against the separation of the economy and culture: 'Political economy is cultural and culture is economic' (1997: 154). For Young, questions of economic equality are central to recognition struggles, for example, 'Many who promote the cultivation of African-American identity [...] do so on the grounds that self-organisation and solidarity in predominately African-American neighbourhoods will improve the material lives of those who live there by providing services and jobs' (2008: 90). Moreover, Young argues that Fraser's dichotomous model is deeply contradictory:

> She treats all instances of group-based claims to cultural specificity and recognition as though recognition is an end in itself. For the movements that Fraser is most concerned with,

> however, – namely, women's movements, movements of people of color, gay and lesbian movements, movements of poor and-working class people – a politics of recognition functions more as a means to, or an element in, broader ends of social and economic equality, rather than as a distinct goal of justice.
>
> Young (2008: 101)

Young (2008) asserts that it is impossible to separate conflict between cultural groups from structural struggles over jobs, land and resources. She concludes:

> Fraser is wrong to conceptualise struggles for recognition of cultural specificity as contradicting struggles for radical transformation of economic structures. So long as the cultural denigration of groups produces or reinforces structural economic oppressions, the two struggles are continuous.
>
> Young (2008: 104–105)

Like Young, Judith Butler argues that the cultural and the economic cannot be separated. Butler contends that Fraser downplays sexuality politics in labelling them as 'merely cultural'. For Butler, the regulation of sexuality is intrinsically tied to the political economy. Fraser and Butler's arguments on sexual politics are considered in detail below wherein I explore recognition debates as they are specifically related to gender and sexuality. Echoing Young, Butler (1998) refutes Fraser's analytical separation of the economic and the cultural, proposing instead an anti-dualistic model. Reflecting on empirical studies of recognition struggles and social movements, Barbara Hobson (2003) also argues for an intersectional analysis of the material and the cultural: '[t]o pose the question that way is to ignore the dynamic interplay between claims to alter maldistribution and challenges to the devaluation of members of a group based on their identities' (Hobson, 2003: 1). Against Fraser's dualist model, Hobson suggests that 'recognition and redistribution become specific lenses for viewing the same struggles, rather than discrete categories' (2003: 2). Anne Phillips concurs, suggesting that 'the more we examine social and political movements, the more intertwined the recognition and redistribution questions appear' (2003: 269).

In their co-authored book *Redistribution or Recognition?* (2003), Fraser and Honneth expressly debate the relationship between the economic and the cultural. Honneth too cautions against Fraser's detachment of material and cultural realms. For Honneth, recognition stands as the core normative category of a theory of social justice; all matters of redistribution can – and should – be considered as matters of redistribution (Thompson, 2006). His argument is threefold: that the sharing (or not) of resources is interlinked with cultural values; that the form of the division of labour and labour status is underpinned by cultural values; that redistribution struggles are informed by cultural interpretations. Culture, then, according to Honneth is central to the political economy: '[i]t is not advisable to theoretically isolate purely economic or systemic factors from cultural elements with regard to the capitalist economic order' (2003: 156). Within political theory, the arenas most frequently analysed in relation to politics of identity (recognition) rather than of redistribution are those relating to sexuality and gender. The next section of this chapter thus explores work that has focused on these sites; arguing for a material/cultural intersectional analysis.

Recognising sexual and gendered inequalities

In 'From Redistribution to Recognition? Dilemma's of Justice in a "Postsocialist Age"' (1995) Fraser focuses on feminist and sexual social movements as examples of 'pure' recognition politics (Young, 2008). Unlike class, which Fraser defines as 'a mode of social differentiation that is rooted in the political – economic structure of society' (2008: 20), sexuality is entirely cultural: 'I treat sexual differentiation as rooted wholly in the cultural structure, as opposed to in the political economy' (2008: 21). Because the class position of lesbians and gay men is various – as a group they may occupy working and middle class strata of the class system – Fraser positions them not as an exploited class but as a collective whose inequalities lie in society's 'cultural-valuation structure' (2008: 21). This leads Fraser to argue that 'the injustice they suffer is quintessentially a matter of recognition' (2008: 21). She continues: 'Gays and lesbians suffer from heterosexism: the authoritative construction of norms that privilege heterosexuality. Their sexuality thus disparaged, homosexuals are subject to shaming, harassment, discrimination, and violence, while being denied legal rights and equal protection – all fundamentally denials of recognition' (2008: 21). Yet, as if to pre-empt her critics, Fraser clarifies:

> To be sure, gays and lesbians also suffer serious economic injustices; they can be summarily dismissed from work and are denied family-based social-welfare benefits. But far from being rooted directly in the economic structure, these derive instead from an unjust cultural-valuation structure. The remedy for the injustice, consequently, is recognition, not redistribution. Overcoming homophobia and heterosexism requires changing the cultural valuations (as well as their legal and practical expressions) that privilege heterosexuality, deny equal respect to gays and lesbians, and refuse to recognize homosexuality as a legitimate way of being sexual. It is to revalue a despised sexuality, to accord positive recognition to gay and lesbian sexual specificity.
>
> Fraser (2008: 22)

Moreover, Fraser explicitly differentiates between politics of sexuality and those of class: 'When we deal with collectivities that approach the ideal type of the exploited working class, we face distributive injustices requiring redistributive remedies. When we deal with collectivities that approach the ideal type of the despised sexuality, in contrast, we face injustices of misrecognition requiring remedies of recognition' (2008: 22). On insisting on the separation of recognition and redistribution, however, Fraser becomes knot tied Indeed, Fraser concedes that:

> Matters become murkier, however, once we move away from these extremes. When we consider collectivities located in the middle of the conceptual spectrum, we encounter hybrid modes that combine features of the exploited class with features of the despised sexuality. These collectivities are 'bivalent'. They are differentiated as collectivities by virtue of *both* the political–economic structure *and* the cultural-valuation structure of society. When disadvantaged, therefore, they suffer injustices that are traceable to both the political economy and culture simultaneously. Bivalent collectivities, in sum, may suffer both socioeconomic maldistribution and cultural recognition in forms where neither of these injustices is an indirect effect of the other, but where both are primate

> and co-original. In that case, neither redistributive remedies alone nor recognition remedies alone will suffice. Bivalent collectivities need both.
>
> Fraser (2008: 22–23)

Fraser also identifies gender and race as bivalent collectivities, which require both redistributive and recognition solutions: 'Both gender and "race", in sum, are dilemmatic modes of collectivity' (2008: 27). Accordingly, gender and race operate as structural principles of the political economy (Fraser, 2008). The thorny question here, though, is which collectivities *do not* emerge from injustices rooted in both the material and cultural? Even Fraser's 'ideal' redistributive category of class is evidently complicated by contingent factors: race, gender, sexuality, disability, age, which, in turn, interweave. Since Fraser acknowledges that gender is a bivalent category: 'It contains a political–economic face that brings it within the ambit of redistribution. Yet it also contains a cultural-valuation face that brings it simultaneously within the ambit of recognition' (2008: 24), it is impossible to see how Fraser can analyse class as a redistributive ideal type in the first instance. Unless, that is, Fraser is applying the category of gender only to women: thus the white working class trade union member stands as the authentic redistributive subject since he is unmarked by gender. Theorists of masculinity have, however, long since theorised masculinity as a hegemonic construct which, as well as offering privilege, is detrimental to, and for, both men and women (Connell, 1995). With this in mind, Fraser's argument is paradoxical throughout.

As discussed above, Young (1997) and Butler (1998) dispute Fraser's partitioning analysis of the political economy and culture. For both, the problematics of this are especially apparent in Fraser's theorisation of sexuality. While Fraser grants gender, alongside race, redistributive qualities, sexuality is 'wholly' – or as Butler reads it, 'merely' – cultural. For Young, this 'trivializes the politics of those oppressed because of their sexuality'. Young's argument here is important:

> Whatever the 'roots' of heterosexism, and I would theorise them as multiple, this harm matters because those on the wrong side of the heterosexual matrix experience systematic limits to their freedom, constant risk of abuse, violence, death, and unjustly limited access

> to resources and opportunities. Among the primary political goals of gay, lesbian, bisexual, transsexual or queer activists are material, economic and political equality [...].
>
> Young (2008: 101–102)

At this point, as will be explored in detail in Chapter 7, Young interpolates her theory of a politics of difference to accomplish material and cultural equality. Her intention, subsequently, is to 'reconnect issues of political economy with issues of recognition. We should show how recognition is a means to, or an element in, economic and political economy' (2008: 101). There are clear parallels here with intersectional theory. Intersectional theory has a long tradition of analysing the ways in which patterns of inequality systematically interweave along the axes of gender, race and class (Hill-Collins, 1990) and, more recently, has broadened to examine sexuality (Taylor, Hines and Casey, 2011). Thus intersectionality has much to offer the redistribution/recognition debate, offering an analytical model through which to theorise what Fraser terms 'murkier' collectivities, or what Young (2008) considers 'unruly categories' – and hence their relationship to each other.

Butler (1998) too strongly disputes Fraser's relegation of sexuality to the cultural realm, stating that this move considers sexuality 'inessential to what is most pressing in material life' (2008: 48). Butler shows how feminist struggles highlighted the ways in which gender and heterosexuality connect to insist that gendered labour divisions were maintained through the reproduction of heterosexuality and the family: 'Thus the regulation of sexuality was systematically tied to the *mode of production* proper to the functioning of political economy' (2008: 58, italics in original). Here, sexuality, alongside gender, is material in functioning the sexual division of labour and reproducing normative ideals of the family:

> Is there any way to analyze how normative heterosexuality and its 'genders' are produced within the sphere of reproduction without noting the compulsory ways in which homosexuality and bisexuality, as well as transgender, are *produced* as the sexually 'abject', and extending the mode of production to account for precisely this social mechanism of regulation? It would be a mistake to understand such productions as 'merely cultural' if they are essential to the functioning of the sexual order of political

> economy, that is, constituting a fundamental threat to its very workability.
>
> Butler (2008: 52–53)

In Butler's analysis, then, modes of sexual production sustain the coherence of gender, heterosexuality and the family, and render unintelligible other modes of being. As Mandy Merk (2007) points out, this argument has long been made by scholars from gender and sexuality studies. Merk remembers the work of Jeffrey Weeks linking male prostitution to the growth of capitalism; of John D'Emilio on capitalist commodification of intimacy; of Gayle Rubin on systems of sexual hierarchy and of Lillian Faberman, who linked lesbian partnerships to middle-class women's financial independence. Moreover, a wave of recent empirical work has (re)tied (homo)sexuality to social class and the material (Brown, 2007; Casey, 2007; Taylor, 2007, 2009, 2011, 2012; McDermott, 2011), while Rosemary Hennessy's (2000) *Profit and Pleasure: Sexual Identities in Late Capitalism*, Denis Altman's *Global Sex* (2001) and Jon Binnie's *The Globalisation of Sexuality* (2004) stand as important recent texts through which to explore the production of queer identities through capitalism and globalisation. Through a phenomenological perspective, Lois McNay also draws attention to the ways in which global capitalism works to lock the cultural to the structural and vice versa: 'impersonal forces shape, in a subtle and often indirect fashion, the felt necessities of daily life [...] more areas of social life are subject to systemic forces of regulation and commodification' (2008: 9–10). Hence McNay's entry into recognition debates is to examine how aspects of gendered embodied subjectivity, such as emotions, are mediated through social relations of power, a theme that will be elaborated on in Chapter 7.

Recognising gender diversity in the UK Gender Recognition Act

(Trans)gender recognition as cultural and material

The UK GRA came into law in 2004. The GRA enables transsexual people to apply to the Gender Recognition Panel for a GRC. Successful applicants are then considered legally in their 'acquired' gender – the term used in the Act to refer to the gender in which a person identifies and presents as distinct from the gender that they were registered in at birth. This enables the person to obtain a new birth certificate showing her/his recognised legal gender. In turn, this permits the person to marry someone of the opposite gender, or to form a civil partnership with someone of the same gender, and gives the rights to retire and receive a state pension. The Act states that a person, male or female, who is over the age of 18, may make an application for gender recognition in terms of:

(a) living in the other gender, or
(b) having changed gender under the law of a country or territory outside the United Kingdom (UK 2004 GRA).

The significance of the GRA lies in the challenges to a biological model of gender, which presumes a fixed relationship between 'sex' and gender identity (Hines, 2010). Until 2004, then, UK law saw gender as biologically fixed at birth. Practically this meant that while trans people modified their bodies and physical appearances, changed their names and constructed new social identities, they were unable to change key legal documents. The impact of the rift between self-identity and legal status was far-reaching and bled into all areas of life. This climate disabled legal rights related to work and welfare (for example, pensions and tax rights) and those related to relationships and parenting (for example, next-of-kin status, marriage, partnership recognition and parental responsibility) and impacted upon the social and cultural fabric of everyday life (for example, trans people were often required to use opposite-sex toilets and changing rooms, treated in opposite-sex hospital wards and sent to opposite-sex prisons). Legal non-recognition also brought the psychological – and very tangible – fear of disclosure (so that a trans person may be publicly outed if, for example, they were called by their original name in a public place, such as a doctor's surgery or benefit office). These issues had long been at the forefront of rights-based trans politics, and central to the campaigning agenda of political lobbying organisation 'Press for Change', which, since the early 1990s, had petitioned the UK government for legal recognition and campaigned against the wide-ranging forms of discrimination faced by trans people.

The issues at stake here are clearly both cultural and material. What is more, the cultural and material qualities interlock. The material (redistributive) claims related to rights, benefits and welfare, as discussed above, depend on the social and cultural acknowledgement of gendered identity (recognition). Without such acknowledgement, without such a degree of social and cultural visibility, trans people will literally be misrecognised. As I suggest above, the impacts – the harms – of misrecognition here are psychologically and materially experienced. It is not surprising, then, that 'recognition' was overtly articulated by research participants when they initially reflected on the significance of the GRA.

Logics of gender recognition

The GRA had been law in the United Kingdom for three years when the project 'Gender Diversity, Recognition and Citizenship' began in 2007. While some participants had successfully applied for gender recognition, others had been unsuccessful in their applications and, more still, were deliberating on whether or not to enter into the process. In interviews and focus groups, participants were first asked what 'recognition' meant to them. Frequently the term was linked to the acknowledgement of gender diversity on both a subjective and a collective level. Reflecting this, Benjamin theorised the GRA as offering him:

> Freedom, liberties, rights [...] And, in terms of history, anything that sort of grants liberties to people, who previously have not had the same rights as anybody else can only be a good thing.
>
> (Benjamin, age 33)

In this project, the majority of participants who had received their GRC said that they now felt accepted by society. This was expressed as offering a legitimate position in society, a position that had been previously denied. In this way, Deirdre said: 'before the GRA it was as if you had been denied your real gender' (Deirdre, age 60). Participants directly linked the recognition of an authentic gender to qualities of respect and status: Fleur, for example, said: 'I saw the GRC as a bit of proof, a bit of legal proof and formal proof of proper status basically' (Fleur, age 51). For Charlene, legal sanctioning was also linked to a new legitimate status:

> Transsexuals have gone from being socially unacceptable to being sanctioned by the government. And that makes a big difference for many people. Whereas previously they thought I was some sort of

> crazy, now Parliament is saying I'm perfectly all right, and there are many other people like me, and that's a good thing.
>
> (Charlene, age 55)

Being recognised in law was expressed as providing a long awaited extension of cultural value, which positively shaped psychological well-being. The legal platform had tipped in participants' favour insofar as they were able to sense a renewed self-esteem and vitality. In Amelia's case, such vivacity was particularly evident: 'I do think it's improved the quality of my life to a level I could never have thought possible' (Amelia, age 46). In many participants' narratives, this psychological lift was clear. For some participants, the GRA seemed to permit the formation of both a psychological defence and a legal defence against possible future wrongdoing. In this way, Amelia said: 'The whole idea of the Act is that for me it's almost a psychological... it's a principle, almost to say, "hey, listen, if you do this you're protected"' (Amelia, age 46).

However, most participants also suggested that they were not so naive to think that the law would create total social harmony and indicated that there would be many more battles to fight in relation to citizenship parity. Indeed, there was a big division among participants around whether the GRA would have a positive impact on cultural attitudes and the social acceptance of transgender people. Some participants felt that there would be a 'trickle down' effect, which would enhance trans people's cultural value, and lead towards social acceptance and greater understanding; Sarah, for example, said 'It [the GRA] creates a sense of formality, a sense of acceptance that with time will result in a reduction of prejudice within society as a whole' (Sarah, age 38). Others, however, felt that legal change had little, if no, effect on social attitudes and cultural understanding. As Jo said:

> A lot of people aren't even aware that the GRA even exists. In fact I guess if you asked the person, man or woman in the street, can you tell me something about GRA? They're not going to be able to. So actually some people seem to be quite surprised that you can do this.
>
> (Jo, age 33)

As I discussed in earlier sections of this chapter, theories of recognition operate along three principle modes. The first mode, 'love', will be considered in Chapter 5 when the book turns to consider the impact of the GRA upon affective ties and intimate relationship. The second principle mode of recognition is 'respect'. In writing about a 'politics of universalism', Charles Taylor (1995) draws on the significance of respect: individuals need fundamental rights so that they can safeguard their autonomy. The significance of respect is also apparent in Nancy Fraser's (1995) writing on 'parity of participation': individual rights are significant to achieving equal participation in society. It is Axel Honneth (1995), however, who writes most strongly on the significance of respect for recognition. In fact, Honneth positions legal recognition as central to enabling respect; modern legal systems help bring about reciprocal respect between members of society. To respect others, according to Honneth, is to recognise them as legal persons (1995: 108). As Thompson says, in Honneth's analysis, 'respect can only be shown to others by treating them as bearers of rights; where rights do not exist, no respect is possible' (2006: 49). Later chapters of this book will dispute Honneth's correlation of respect and a legal framework of rights. Indeed, I argue that the GRA exemplifies how a legal framework may impede respect in setting up problematic distinctions of authenticity. Furthermore, the GRA, will be read as producing more stringent forms of regulation and 'conditionality' (Dywer, 2004). In drawing on research findings to empirically evaluate recognition theory, however, the importance of recognition as an enabler of respect reverberates. The participants' narratives above indicate the resonance of respect; in each, recognition is understood as important in bringing about greater societal respect for trans people.

Respect here is also linked to increased legitimisation, rights and status. Such themes dovetail with the third principle of recognition, that of 'esteem'. Esteem positively acknowledges distinctive characteristics of identity, difference, culture or community (Thompson, 2006). As I discussed earlier, running alongside Taylor's (1995) 'politics of universalism' is his notion of a 'politics of difference', to which esteem is an imperative in positively affirming cultural or community values and characteristics. Esteem figures in Honneth's (1995) analysis through a 'politics of solidarity', whereby communities' particular contributions to society are equally valued. For Fraser (1995), esteem is a requirement of 'participatory parity'. Each of these analyses and applications of esteem run through the participants' narratives considered above. Like 'respect', then, 'esteem' was understood by research participants as a vital feature of recognition. Thus, on both the conceptual level – what participants understood recognition to mean – and the subjective level – why recognition mattered to them – research findings support the emphasis placed on the qualities of respect and esteem and, also, protection, rights, benefits and status that, as this chapter has explored, run through theories of recognition.

Conclusion

This chapter began by situating the academic turn to recognition within social, cultural and political changes on national and global levels. A political theory of recognition has been developed to account for the rise of new social movements, which have organised around issues of identity and difference, culture and community, notably as they relate to gender, sexuality, race, ethnicity and embodiment. The chapter then looked in more detail at the principles of recognition as they are addressed in the work of Honneth, Taylor and Fraser, paying particular attention to modes of respect and esteem. Central to recognition theory is the debate around recognition/redistribution. Recognition theorists argue that recent years have seen a move away from collective class-based politics to social movements who espouse a politics of identity. For Fraser, this is read as constituting a move from redistributive to recognition politics. This chapter addressed the debate and, by drawing on the work of Young and Butler in particular, argued for an intersectional analysis of the economic and the cultural.

In order to empirically evaluate this point, the second section of this chapter moved on to address the UK 2004 GRA First I outlined the criteria of the Act and then drew on participants' narratives to explore how recognition was understood. In evaluating the literature through empirical data, I argued that the recognition claims of trans people were both material (redistributive) and cultural (recognition-based). These points will be reconsidered in Chapter 7, where I suggest that a politics of difference is more able to account for transgender intersectionalities than is a politics of recognition. In the last section of this chapter, I examined the ways in which research narratives resonated with the qualities of respect and esteem, as considered in the literature.

Chapter 2 follows on from these debates by mapping the development of transgender claims for recognition. Here I assess the emergence of a transgender movement in relation to Honneth's notion of recognition struggles, as outlined in this chapter. Chapter 2 also makes links back to this chapter in considering the problematics of a politics of identity, or, to use Taylor's term, 'authentic' identities.

2
Moving for Recognition

Introduction

This chapter traces post-1960 claims for recognition based on gender, sexuality and, later, transgender in order to examine themes of connection and disconnection across and between different social movements around gender and sexuality as they moved to claim recognition. The chapter examines the recent histories of gendered and sexual social movement organisation, which, since the 1960s, has set out varied, and often disparate, frameworks for gender and sexual recognition. Social movement organisation has been well documented in relation to the contribution of, and the impact upon, the political cultures of women (Mitchell, 1973; Allen, Sanders and Wallis, 1974; Rowbotham, Segal, Wainwright, 1981; Wilson, 1982; Rowbotham, 2001) and sexual minorities (D'Emilio, 1983, 2004; D'Emilio and Freedman, 1988; Weeks, 2000, 2007; Carter, 2004). Yet the role of trans people in the social transformations that have occurred around gender and sexuality over the last five decades has received scant attention.

Tracing these historical connections – and disconnections – is important both conceptually and politically for considerations of transgender recognition. As I have argued elsewhere (Hines, 2007a), practices of gender diversity raise important questions about the epistemological and ontological status of sex, gender and sexuality. That is, they call into question understandings of, and investments in, binary systems of male/female and hetero/homo. Additionally, trans sexualities do not easily fit with models of bisexuality (Hines, 2007a; see also Cromwell, 1999; Richardson and Monro, 2012). In these ways, transgender brings challenges to issues central to theory and activism around gender and sexuality.

In the absence of an autonomous transgender political movement – and long before the development of transgender studies – trans people made alliances with, and were often central to, feminist and sexual politics. Yet, despite the presence of trans activists in early lesbian and gay movements, the relationship between lesbian and gay and trans politics has often been contentious. Similarly, the relationship between transgender and feminism has been far from smooth (Hines, 2007a, 2010).

The chapter first examines claims for recognition across and between social movements based around gender and sexuality. Next, it moves on to explore the development of political organisation and recognition politics around gender, sexuality and transgender. The last section of the chapter links back to the literate considered in Chapter 1 – first to examine the emergence of a transgender movement through Honneth's (1995) notion of 'recognition struggles' and, second, to consider the problematics of a politics of identity in relation to recognition politics.

Looking back – in anger: Transgender exclusion

'Women's' liberation

Transgender poses thorny questions concerning the constitution of 'sex' and 'gender'. Transgender also problematises a straightforward reading of the relationship between these categories. Thus transgender raises intricate questions about the construction, deconstruction and ongoing reconstruction of both gender and sexual taxonomies (Hines, 2007a, 2010). Reflecting a growing public awareness of Western transgender practices since the 1950s, second-wave feminism was one of the first academic fields to engage with transgender (Hird, 2002; Hines, 2007a); however, the relationship between feminism and transgender has proved contentious. The hostility of some radical feminist writers, particularly evident in the writing of Janice Raymond (1980), and later Sheila Jeffreys (1997) and Julie Bindel (2003), has been well documented in my other work (Hines, 2007a, 2007b, 2010). From the premise that 'it is biologically impossible to change *chromosomal* sex' (Raymond, 1980: 10, italics in the original), Raymond rebuffed the feminist politics of trans women. On the place of trans women within feminism, biology was inserted as precursor for female identity, and so for a feminist politics of identity: 'the man who undergoes sex conversion is *not* female' (1980: 10, italics in original). The central issue of contestation for these writers, then, was the relationship between biological sex and gender, and the subsequent implications for the status of 'woman' – and thus of feminism. Yet the status of female biology disappeared in debates surrounding the role of trans men in feminist communities, and it is gender identity – that of male – not biology or gender socialisation – that is drawn upon here to distance trans people from feminism.

A very vocal strand of feminist theory and recognition politics has therefore assumed a stable identity – understood through the category of 'woman'. 'Woman' not only initiates feminist interests and goals here, but constitutes the subject for whom recognition is pursued (Hines, 2007a; 2010). From this premise, trans women and men have been positioned as outsiders at discursive and political levels. Autobiographical writing by trans activists (Stone, 1991; Bornstein, 1994; Feinberg, 1996; Riddell, 1996; Califia, 1997; Wilchins, 1997) shows the personal and political effects of these othering practices. My empirical research has also illustrated the ways in which trans women and trans men found themselves excluded from feminist communities (Hines, 2005, 2006a, 2007a). This body of work indicates that transgender was far from a peripheral issue within feminist debates of the 1980s and 1990s. Rather, the relationship between transgender and feminism occupied a central place at the debating table, as indicated by Leslie Feinberg's insistence that 'the development of the trans movement has raised a vital question that's being discussed in women's communities all over the country. How is woman defined? The answer we give may determine the course of women's liberation for decades to come' (1996: 109). My previous research has pointed to more positive interactions between current feminist and trans communities (see Hines, 2007a); however, continued tensions at both theoretical and activist levels resound in contemporary recognition debates.

Several scholars have written productively on the connections between transgender and feminism (Wilchins, 1997; Hale, 1998; Rubin, 1998; Cromwell, 1999; Monro, 2000, 2004; Koyama, 2003; Monro and Warren, 2004; Hines, 2005), tracing links particularly around the politics of bodily autonomy and the critical examination of gender roles. Henry Rubin's writing on the intersections between feminism and transgender is especially salient for moving away from a politics of identity in order to create political bonds. In Rubin's analysis, feminist identity arises out of political commitment rather than female biology: '"Womanhood" is no longer a necessary, nor sufficient qualification for feminist identity. A feminist is one who acts in concert with feminist ideals' (Rubin, 1998: 308). Accordingly, political practice, rather than biology or gender socialisation, is the feminist motivator. Here on in, feminist analyses of embodiment may be developed without essentialist connotations in order to account for 'differently located bodies which appear similar in form' (Rubin, 1998: 308). For Rubin, this enables a 'way of knowing that can provide me(n) with a feminist viewpoint, and that is not generated out of a woman's experience of her body. Instead, it is generated out of subjectively located struggle' (Rubin, 1998: 308). In turn, I have suggested that feminist politics be uncoupled from 'female socialisation' to connect feminism and trans femininity (Hines, 2005; 2007a). I will flesh out this argument towards the end of this chapter in looking at debates within the recognition literature around authentic identities and the problematics of a politics of identity. Moreover, Rubin's arguments are, I believe, significant for conceptualising a politics of difference, which I explore in detail in Chapter 7. Here, though, I move on to examine the dynamics around transgender in relation to sexual social movements, which illustrate very similar areas of contestation around recognition that have been drawn out in the above discussion concerning feminism and transgender.

Sexual liberation

Historically there is much to connect transgender and lesbian and gay activism. Yet the role of trans people in landmark events within sexual politics has often been obscured in the accounts of sexual historians. As Devor and Matte suggest: ' [P]eople who are today known as transgendered and transsexual have always been present in homosexual rights movements. Their presence and contributions, however, have not always been fully acknowledged or appreciated' (Devor and Matte, 2006: 387). Susan Stryker's work serves to rectify this in evidencing the activism of trans people in key moments such as 'Compton's Cafeteria' riot in 1968 and the more infamous 'Stonewall Riots' a year later.

Compton's Cafeteria in the Tenderloin district of San Francisco was an all-night meeting point for sex workers and homeless people. It was also one of the few places in San Francisco where trans people felt able to be publicly visible. Throughout the 1950s and 1960s, cross-dressing was illegal in California and transgender people were unwelcome in most gay bars (Stryker, 2008). In her 2005 documentary *Screaming Queens*, Stryker locates the Compton's Cafeteria riots as the starting point for a new type of politics led by gender and sexual minorities:

> It's a hot August night in San Francisco in 1966 – three years before the famed Stonewall. Compton's Cafeteria, in the seedy Tenderloin district, is hopping with its usual assortment of transgender people, young street hustlers, and down-and-out regulars. The management, annoyed by the noisy crowd at one table, calls the police. When a surly cop, accustomed to manhandling Compton's clientele, attempts to arrest one of the queens, she throws her coffee in his face. Mayhem erupts – windows break, furniture flies through the air. Police reinforcements arrive, and the fighting spills into the street. For the first time, the drag queens band together to fight back, getting the better of the cops, whom they kick and stomp with their high-heeled shoes and beat with their heavy purses. For everyone at Compton's that night, one thing was certain – things would never be the same again.
>
> Stryker comptonscafeteriariot.org

Following the riot, trans people were barred from entering Compton's, leading to frequent, and often violent, pickets. According to Stryker, the aftermath of the riot marked a turning point in the Lesbian, Gay, Bisexual and Transgender (LGBT) movement:

> It was the first time that people who were discriminated against because of their gender identity banded together to resist their oppression. And it had results. In the years after the riot, trans activists and allies began to make real progress in meeting the unique social and medical needs of trans people.
>
> Stryker comptonscafeteriariot.org

The New York Stonewall riots, a year after those of Compton's, have become synonymous with the birth of the modern lesbian and gay movement. While such a mythological positioning of Stonewall is contentious (Murray, 1996) and, certainly, lesbian and gay political organisations had existed in preceding decades – most notably in the 1950s with the 'Mattachine Society' and the 'Daughters of Bilitis' – it is widely agreed by sexual historians (D'Emilio, 1983; Weeks, 2000) that Stonewall marked a significant political shift. Earlier lesbian and gay organisations were largely conservative about the route to social change (Weeks, 2000); their goal was to work within the existing system to organise for recognition. The civil rights, black power, anti-war and women's movements of the mid- to late 1960s, however, inspired a more militant politics in younger lesbian and gay activists. As John D'Emilio (1983) discusses, raids on the 'Stonewall Inn' were nothing new. In 1969, though, New York was in the middle of a mayoral campaign and the clean-up of the bar took on a new impetus. It operated without a liquor license and had ties to organised crime. It was popular with black and Hispanic gay men, trans women and drag queens, and, as D'Emilio remarks: 'offering scantily clad go-go boys as entertainment, it brought an "unruly" element to Sheridan Square' (D'Emilio, 1983: 231). In D' Emilio's account of Stonewall, the events of 28 June are distinguished from previous raids by both the size and the anger of the reacting clientele. The riots lasted for five days and a crowd of, according to David Carter's (2004) research, around 2,000 protesters continued to fight back at attempts to arrest them.

In most retellings of Stonewall, it is trans woman Sylvia Rivera who is identified as initiating the Stonewall uprising by throwing a bottle at police. Rivera became a member of the 'Gay Activists Alliance' and a founding member of the 'Gay Liberation Front'. Yet – and herein lies my point for recounting these events in detail – in the years following Stonewall, Rivera found herself excluded from these sexual movements. As she said in an interview in 1995: 'when things started getting more mainstream [...] it was like, "we don't need you no more" ' (quoted in Wilchins, 1997). Matt Foreman, the executive director of the National Gay and Lesbian Task Force in the United States, reflects:

> There was a time when nobody wanted to even mention transgender issues or have transgender people accompany you on lobbying visits to members of your state assembly because that

> was pushing the envelope too far [...] There was a myth in our community, and frankly I was part of that myth, that including transgender people would set our cause back.
>
> Quoted in Leff (2012)

Foreman's narrative explicitly illustrates the exclusion of trans people from lesbian and gay organisations. Processes of distancing, and practices of exclusion, are thus starkly apparent in historical relationships between trans people and gender and sexual social movements. Trans people's claims for recognition – as lesbian or gay themselves, or as political allies – were accordingly refuted. Nevertheless, as the next section of this chapter details, personal and political alienation from these movements provided the impetus for the development of a politics of transgender recognition.

Pressing for change: Transgender recognition

While a feminist politics of recognition was dependent upon the category 'woman', claims for sexual recognition by lesbian and gay men were based around the articulation of experiences of alienation because of same-sex desire and identity. Problematically for trans people, same-sex sexual identity categories were understood through a gendered lens: so that a lesbian identity mapped onto a female body and a gay male identity was a product of male embodiment (Hines, 2007a). Moreover, sexual identity categories did not simply denote the gender of the identifying subject, but also that of her/his object of desire: thus a 'lesbian' desired 'women' and a 'gay man' desired 'men' (Hines, 2010). Such straightforward readings of the relationship between gender and sexuality have been problematised through transgender scholarship and autobiography (Devor, 1989; Feinberg, 1996; Nataf, 1996; Halberstam, 1998; Cromwell, 1999; Monro, 2005; Boyd, 2006; Devor and Matte, 2006; Schrock and Reid, 2006; Stryker and Whittle, 2006; Hines, 2007a, 2010; Sanger, 2008; Davy, 2010). As transgender complicated understandings of gender as coherent, so it problematised the notion of sexual identity as unitary. As Devor and Matte argue:

> transgendered and transsexual people destabilize the otherwise easy divisions of men and women into categories of straight

> and gay because they are both and/or neither. Thus there is a long standing tension over the political terrain of queer politics between gays and lesbians, on the one hand, and transgendered and transsexual people, on the other.
>
> Devor and Matte (2006)

Throughout the 1990s, a number of trans activists called for alliances between lesbian and gay and trans political organisations (Feinberg, 1996) at the same time as building autonomous political and support-based communities. Through the emergence of what Stryker terms 'politicized communities of identity' (Stryker, 2006: 5), a distinct transgender politics of recognition surfaced in the formation of US activist groups such as 'Transgender Nation and FtM International', community cultural productions such as zines *Gender Trash* and *The Transsexual News Telegraph* and trans community activism around, for example, AIDS. In the United Kingdom, the transgender political lobbying group Press for Change (PfC) was formed after Mark Rees lost his case for rights to privacy and marriage in the European Court of Human Rights (ECHR). The decade also witnessed the growth of trans support groups and community networks of care (Hines, 2007b). As the next section of the chapter explores, these practices of community building and care went hand-in-hand with political organisation and claims for recognition, which, in time, resulted in significant legal change.

Demanding rights, enacting change

Overarching themes of connection emerge in narrating the development of feminist, lesbian and gay, and transgender social movements and respective claims for social and political recognition. Each movement emerged to challenge cultures of social and material marginalisation, instances of disadvantage and practices of discrimination. Each utilised a specific identity – 'woman', 'lesbian', 'gay', 'trans' – as an identity marker through which to share experience and articulate a politics of recognition. More problematically, each defended 'their' identity against that of 'others' in pursuit of political recognition. It is from this juncture that the chapter moves on to consider issues that have been central to gender and sexual movements since the 1960s. Here I am concerned with examining the impacts of feminism, sexual politics and trans movements on law and policy.

Gender politics

Recent autobiographical writing by feminist activists highlights the sexism at play within the Left-based liberation movements of the 1960s (DuPlessis and Snitow, 1998; Rowbotham, 2001; Segal, 2007). These issues resonate strongly with debates among political theorists around the supposed move on the Left from a focus on class to one on gender, race and sexuality, as discussed in Chapter 1. Issues central to women's lives – inequality and low pay in the workforce, domestic labour, childcare, sexual autonomy and safety – were sidelined within the political Left. Some male activists – and political theorists, see the attitudes of Rorty (2000) and Barry (2001) outlined in Chapter 1, – argued that a focus upon women's issues was divisive; that it would dissipate attention from the 'real' cause – class revolution. Furthermore, it was not only women's 'issues' that were marginalised: women activists were often relegated to the periphery by male activists who saw their role in the movement as predominately a supportive one. Sheila Rowbotham remembers a meeting with the collective of the Left magazine *Black Dwarf*: 'he (the male activist) simply assumed it was the men's job to talk politics. [...] he sent me off to the bedroom to stuff envelopes with the other women' (Rowbotham, 2000: 177). As Lynne Segal states, these experiences of marginalisation were the impetus for a burgeoning women's movement:

> *after* working with our 'brothers' to oppose the evils of the Vietnam war, *after* supporting workers in the struggle in an era of trade union militancy, *after*, above all, seeing ourselves the hip chick of the 60s sexual liberation, facing ever cruder sexist pin-ups and porn in the underground press, confronting the sexism of our comrades – after this, many women glimpsed that we needed a bit of liberation of our own. And that was the birth of women's liberation.
>
> Segal quoted in Weeks (2007: 18)

Women activists subsequently met separately in workshops and consciousness raising groups. Speaking about the United States, Jo Freeman recalled:

> For months they met quietly to analyze their perpetual secondary roles in the radical movement, assimilate lessons learned in study groups, or reflect on their treatment in the civil rights movement. They were constantly ridiculed by the men they worked with and continually told that what they were doing was 'counter-revolutionary' because it would further splinter an already badly fragmented movement. In many ways this very ridicule served to feed their growing rage. One immediate result was that all the groups independently banned men from their meetings.
>
> Freeman (1971: 150)

Women's groups thus developed as spaces where women organised for a politics of recognition based on both economic (redistributive) and cultural (recognition) issues: childcare, reproductive rights, cultural representation, sexual violence, and low pay and discrimination in the workplace – issues that became central to feminist demands over the next decades and led to the development of new law and policy to protect for women's interests across these cultural and material spheres. Importantly, feminism also worked to conceptually challenge understandings of gender by problematising dominant understandings of the role of women in key institutions such as the family, heterosexual relations, health care and the workplace. Indeed, feminism directly spelt out the ways in which these spheres acted *as* institutions, which strategically shaped the lives of women.

Central to feminist activism was the notion that the personal is political. This problematised dichotomies of public/private and brought issues such as sexuality, cultural representation and safety on the street into the political arena, again drawing attention to the intersections of the cultural and the material in these recognition claims. Here it is important to recall the areas of connection between feminism and sexual politics. Many women were involved in both movements as feminists and as lesbians, while other lesbians broke away from sexual political groups to become part of the women's movement. There were also clear connections between areas of activism in each movement around, for example, discrimination in the workplace, public health provision, street safety and cultural representation.

Sexual politics

The criminalisation of homosexuality in the United Kingdom until 1967 is perhaps the clearest way of illustrating the extent to which same-sex desire and practice was deviantly positioned in UK 20th and early 21st society. As Diane Richardson and Surya Monro write:

> Those growing up in the 1950s, for instance, lived through a time when homosexuality was defined as abnormal, unnatural and inferior to heterosexuality. Generally regarded as a medical disorder and as social deviance, homosexuality was seen as posing a direct threat to social and moral order that the state and other institutions sought to contain through criminalisation and other measures.
>
> Richardson and Monro (2012: 20)

The emergence of a sexual politics of recognition thus spoke directly to the law. Following high-profile cases in which men, such as Oscar Wilde, were imprisoned for homosexuality, groups of (largely) men began to meet – first in secret and then more openly – to campaign for legal change. Early groups such as the 'homophile movement' were conservative in their demands, articulating recognition in the same language as that by which they were medically disqualified (Foucault, 1979). While some seeked 'tolerance' on the grounds of biological or psychic disorder (Foucault, 1979), others spoke against pathologisation by arguing that they were the *same as* heterosexuals (Richardson and Seidman, 2002; Richardson and Monro, 2012). Following the decriminalisation of homosexuality in 1967, the claims on which recognition were based became bolder, the voice of 'appeal' turned to statements of 'demand'. Yet, as Chapter 4 addresses, rather than diminishing, a language of sexual recognition based on 'sameness' remains the language of many rights-based political claims, and, by turn, is strongly contested by other sections of gender- and sexuality-based social movements.

Echoing the politics of feminism, then, sexual movements of the 1970s focused on both redistribution and recognition politics. As discussed above, the 'Stonewall Riots' paved the way for a more radical sexual politics, evident in the formation of the *Gay Liberation Front* in 1970 (see Adam, 1992; Weeks, 2007). Assimilationist ideals – or a politics of 'sameness' – coexisted with a celebration of difference, the latter articulated through the notion of gay *pride*. Lesbian political organisations developed autonomously to address the specific intersections of gender and sexuality (D'Emilio and Freedman, 1998) and, as will be discussed in Chapter 5, the significance of class and race in experiences of sexuality became politicised. Trans people, though, remained on the margins of sexual political movements. Bisexuals also found themselves displaced by both feminist and lesbian and gay movements (Monro, 2005; Richardson and Monro, 2012), and bisexual communities later developed independently at grassroots levels (Hemmings, 2002; Richardson and Monro, 2012).

The devastating impact of HIV and AIDS on gay communities in the 1980s led to the formation of organisations such as 'Outrage' in the United Kingdom and 'ACT UP' in the United States. So emerged a politics of fury: at the lack of medical research into HIV and AIDS, at limited access to health care and medicine and at the explicitly homophobic language of the Regan (United States) and Thatcher (United Kingdom) Governments in debates around HIV and AIDS, which fuelled homophobia in the media and on the street. As women's groups found support and articulated a politics of the 'personal' through consciousness raising groups, communities affected by HIV and AIDS came together to develop their own practices of care. As Barry Adam writes:

> Care, organized by community-based AIDS groups, includes a wide range of professional services, from counselling and legal assistance to food banks and therapeutic support, but it is also of the most mundane sort: running errands, house sitting, cat feeding, being there, nursing and all the realm of domestic labour.
>
> Adam (1992: 81)

Jeffrey Weeks, Brain Heaphy and Catherine Donovan (2001) also document community-based practices of care: 'ostracised groups of black people, women and haemophiliacs, as well as gay men, developed distinct practices of care, which fit with the notion of community as a site of identity and resistance' (Weeks et al., 2001: 90). Several writers speak of how HIV/AIDS re-motivated sexual politics and refocused organisation around welfare and policy (Watney, 1994; Epstein, 1999; Richardson, 2005; Richardson and Monro, 2012). As Richardson and Monro (2012) discuss, political organisation around HIV and AIDS was important in giving impetus to international organisation around sexual politics – as will be discussed in Chapter 3 in relation to the globalisation of sexuality, and human rights discourse and law.

While legal and policy change remained of central concern – for example, in relation to HIV and AIDS, and issues such as the age of consent, 'Clause 28' in the United Kingdom, and parenting and partnering rights – legal advances were slow to come by: in the United Kingdom gay men were not allowed to serve openly in the military until 2000; the age of consent remained unequal until 2001; same-sex partnerships were not recognised until 2004 (Civil Partnership Act (CPA, 2004)); parity of adoption law did not exist until 2006 (Children and Adoption Act, 2006) and discrimination on the grounds of sexuality in the workplace was not addressed in law until 2007 (Equality Act, 2007). These legal developments will be discussed in detail in Chapter 6.

Transgender politics

Organisation for transgender legal recognition developed much later than feminist and sexuality-based politics, though support groups and self-help organisations for trans people emerged in the 1960s, and both multiplied and diversified in following decades (see Hines, 2007a). Although support groups and, later, transgender charitable organisations did not lobby government for legal or policy change, their goal was political in seeking to enact social and cultural change through community education programmes focusing on transgender issues and providing local government and services with advice on best practice when dealing with transgender clients. Central to the aims of support groups was the elimination of guilt and shame, and, here, transgender support groups linked with the goals of the lesbian and gay movement in the late 1960s and early 1970s to enable 'an affirmation of a positive sense of self and of the collective means of realising this' (Weeks et al., 2001: 14). Similarities can also be drawn between initiatives of care and support by and for transgender people and the practices of care developed by and for communities affected by HIV and AIDS in the 1980s and 1990s (Adam, 1992; Weeks et al., 2001), which, again, show how marginalised communities develop as a site of identity and resistance (Weeks et al., 2001: 90).

The formation of PfC in 1992 in the United Kingdom signified a move towards organisation for legal change, as PfC's founding statement indicates: 'seeking respect and equality for all trans people in the United Kingdom, through case law, legislation, and social change' (http://www.pfc.org.uk/index.html). Primarily a voluntary organisation, PfC provides legal advice and equality training on transgender rights for public and private bodies. Moreover, PfC worked closely with government on transgender rights as they related to the Employment Regulations (1999), the GRA (2004) and the Equality Act (2010). The Equality Act (2010) is central to the focus in Chapter 6 on post-1997 UK equalities and diversity policy and law around gender and sexuality. Chapter 6 will return to consider the role of transgender campaigning organisations in effecting legal change in this instance.

Recognition struggles

The idea that recognition only emerges through struggle has long been narrated. One of the first explanations of recognition struggles is Hegel's (1807) description of master/slave dynamics. Jean-Paul Sartre (1943) also used the notion of recognition struggle in his account of anti-Semitism, while Frantz Fanon (1952) employed the term in discussing the relationship between the colonialised and the colonialiser. In these accounts, the oppressed subject must fight for equality – for recognition. The notion of recognition struggles is also widespread within political theory to characterise politics of identity; here the marginalised subject struggles for recognition of difference.

Struggles for recognition are central to Axel Honneth's (1995) theory of recognition. Struggle denotes conflict and, according to Honneth, this conflict becomes apparent when subjects demand the recognition they are denied. Through struggles for recognition, society achieves what Honneth writes about as its 'ideal state'. In other words, recognition struggles bring about social justice. As discussed in Chapter 1, Honneth positions the law as one vehicle for enabling social justice. The law chamber is positioned as a site through which recognition is claimed on a journey of moral progress. To step back a little, Honneth's first point of call on the journey from conflict to justice is 'hurt feelings' (1995: 1963) – the term used by Honneth to describe emotions such as shame, sadness or anger, which arise from social exclusion. In turn, as discussed in Chapter 1, a subject's self-respect and self-esteem are weakened. Hurt feelings derive from injustice, from a lack of recognition. Honneth proposes that social movements emerge from the transference of individual to collective hurt. So 'private experiences of injury' (1995: 163) are turned into collective demands for justice, thus arising as recognition struggles. Honneth continues to argue that recognition struggles are the drivers of moral progress – moving society, to use Simon Thompson's turn of phrase, 'towards a full realization of undistorted relations of recognition' (2006: 164).

The last part of Honneth's argument – that recognition struggles form the backbone of moral progress – will be assessed in Chapter 3. His consideration of a move from individual hurt to collective struggle, though, is supported in the accounts in this chapter concerning the emergence of social movements around gender, sexuality and transgender. This chapter, has, however, traced the ways in which a politics of identity, as discussed in Chapter 1, has worked to re-marginalise subjects. Thus women were excluded from the Left, though often went on to distance themselves from trans people on the basis of feminist politics which authenticated 'woman'. A very similar story was traced in relation to sexual minorities and their subsequent disengagement with trans people. Importantly, then, the politics of identity that fuel recognition struggles may themselves act as excluding mechanisms. A critique of identity politics as played out in recognition struggles is central to the over-arching argument of this book and is a theme that will re-emerge in subsequent chapters.

Conclusion

This chapter began by looking back, tracing key moments and central themes in recognition narratives of feminist, lesbian, gay and transgender social movements. It has considered the relationship between these movements, taking in moments of connection and disconnection. The work of social movements around gender – and here I am including transgender – and sexuality, has, importantly, not only brought about legal and policy shifts. Activism has increased the social and cultural visibility of non-normative gender and sexual practices and identities and has provided members of these groups with support, care and means of community affiliation. In this way, I argue that these claims are both redistributive and recognition-based. As this chapter charts, as much as a rights-based politics was in evidence in feminist, lesbian and gay and trans communities, so too was a politics of liberation – a politics of liberation that was broad in its scope, taking in the cultural and social, as well as the material, a politics that was visible and vocal in demanding rights and recognition.

Central to the politics – and the political successes – of the social movements considered in this chapter, is the notion of identity. Running through this chapter has been consideration of the ways in which identity was claimed both subjectively and strategically. Identity politics is thus central to rights-based politics and, hence, to a politics of recognition. This is not to suggest, though, that post-war social movements around gender and sexuality have entirely – or even largely – been concerned with legal and policy change. While a politics of identity may alleviate isolation and increase levels of protection, it has not provided parity within or across categories of gender and sexuality. Some women are, of course, more 'equal' (to other groups of women and to other groups of men) than are others, while some members of sexual minorities are more 'recognised' than are others. Such intersectional markers of (in)equality cut through and between the categories of gender and sexuality themselves (Hines, 2010). Issues of intersectionality are, I suggest, central to a politics of difference: a framework for which is developed in Chapter 7.

Claims for equality based on gender and sexual identity have consequently been subject to much theoretical and political critique. Subsequent chapters explore these challenges as they are articulated in debates around the concepts of recognition, human rights, equality and diversity, and citizenship. Moreover, following chapters will explore these challenges at a substantive level by considering critiques of rights-based politics. In considering the impact of an agenda of recognition on broader sections of gender and sexual social movements, it is necessary to take account of individuals and groups who have been less accounted for through a rights-based route to equality. Here, then, the narrative of the book broadens in subsequent chapters to take account of moments of collective failure, as well as successes.

3
Recognition, Misrecognition and Human Rights

Introduction

This chapter contextualises the UK GRA (2004) within human rights discourse and law. As the chapter explores, the GRA could not have been conceived outside of the language of human rights or without a framework for human rights law. Thus it was a deficiency in human rights for transgender people in UK state law that led the ECHR to caution the UK government about the lack of rights for transgender people and a discourse of human rights that carved the way for claims to the ECHR by transgender people. First the chapter examines a series of claims brought by trans people to the ECHR and locates these claims as forming the backdrop to the GRA. Central to each of these claims was the language of 'rights' – in particularly, the right to privacy and the right to family life (as set out in the HRA, 1998). In examining the language and the execution of these recognition claims, the chapter explores the ways in which gender is constructed and reconstructed through discourses and practices of human rights.

The next section of the chapter considers the issues at stake in accounting for gender and sexual transformations through a framework of human rights. Here I address the problematics of universalism, which, the chapter argues, are inherent in human rights language and claims and are rehearsed in the recognition literature, as discussed in Chapter 1. Problems with claims for recognition based on universalism will be examined at European and global levels. Here, I illustrate a number of ways in which a politics of recognition can, paradoxically, instate instances of misrecognition with alarming consequences. Such issues resonate with discussions of equalities and diversity policy in Chapter 6 and are central to this book's critique of identity politics.

Claiming recognition through human rights

Human rights are considered as basic rights and freedoms to which all human beings are entitled. They are set out through the international standards of the Universal Declaration of Human Rights (UDHR), which the UK signed up to in 1948, and applied through the *European Convention of Human Rights*. There are now nine international human rights instruments, which protect the rights of particular groups (Waites, 2009). While 'citizenship' denotes the rights and responsibilities of 'belonging' to a particular state, citizenship's status within human rights discourse is often centrally positioned so that citizenship rights are seen as key to broader human rights. From this premise, the *Commission for Equality and Human Rights* states that 'citizenship is a human rights issue. Many rights cannot be expressed unless secured by citizenship' (equalityhumanrights.com). These qualities, as Chapter 1 examined, run through recognition theory. Similarly, the human rights principles of autonomy and dignity echo with the emphasis placed on respect and esteem in the work of the recognition theorists addressed in Chapter 1.

Each of these legal developments arose from the recognition struggles of gender and sexual movements, as discussed in Chapter 2, and each intersect the cultural and the material (redistribution and recognition), as discussed in Chapter 1. Moreover, new legislation in the United Kingdom aimed at inequalities based on gender and sexuality follows on from the HRA (1998), specifically *Article 8: the right to respect for private and family life; Article 12: the right to marry and found a family* and *Article 14: prohibition of discrimination.* The passing of the HRA itself was part of post-1997 culture in which notions of 'equality', 'rights' and 'citizenship' became articulated anew. As later sections of the chapter illustrate, there is also a direct relationship between policy and legal developments at the European level and UK policy changes. It is also clear that the UK GRA (2004) developed as a result of criticism about the lack of recognition for transgender people in the United Kingdom from the ECHR.

Human rights law and the Gender Recognition Act

Before the UK (GRA 2004), Britain was one out of four European countries that failed to legally recognise the acquired gender of transsexual people (Whittle, 2002). In enabling transgender people to change their birth certificates and to marry, the GRA marks a sea change in sociolegal attitudes to gender. As I have argued elsewhere (Hines, 2007a), this represents a move towards the separation of 'gender' and 'sex' – an argument that has also been put forward by Cowan (2005) and Sandland (2005). Rather than biological 'sex' being the marker of identity, 'gender' recognises that identity is more fluidly experienced and practised (Hines, 2009). Petitions to the ECHR by transgender people were instrumental to the development of the GRA. In order to examine the backdrop of the GRA, then, the chapter proceeds to examine three cases that petitioned for the rights of transgender people through international human rights law.

In the case of X, Y and Z, in 1997, a transgendered man (X) took his case to ECHR to be recognised as the father of the child (Z) of his female partner (Y), who had conceived through donor insemination. He cited Article 8, the right to respect for private and family life, of the HRA (1998): 'Everyone has a right to respect for his private and family life, his home and his correspondence' (the HRA, 1998), and Article 14, the prohibition of discrimination: 'The enjoyment of the rights and freedoms set forth in the convention shall be secured without discrimination on any ground such as sex, race, colour, language, religion, political or other opinion, national or social origin, association with a national minority, property, birth or other status' (the HRA, 1998). While the court decided that Article 8 was applicable to the case, they judged that the law was in transition since there is no standardised judgement among European states of council as to whether non-biological fathers should be granted parental rights. Further, the court believed that the issues raised by non-biological transgendered parents were too complex for Article 8 to be upheld. In relation to Article 14, the court stated that the complainant repeated the same issues as the complaint to Article 8 and that, as such, it need not be considered under Article 14.

Although the case was lost, there was dissent among the judges. One judge argued that not to allow X to appear on the birth certification of the children was discrimination on the grounds of sex as set out in Article 14 and, as such, that family ties were not being respected as set out in Article 8. Crucially, another judge argued that since the UK government had not proved that they would ensure the legal recognition of X's gender reassignment, they were in violation of both Articles 8 and 14. It was argued that the law should be reviewed to take account of social and medical developments.

A year later, in 1998, the case of Sheffield & Horsham was heard in the ECHR. The two transgendered women appealed under Articles 8 and 14. Although the case was lost, again, the lack of legal recognition of gender transition in the United Kingdom was critically highlighted by judges: 'Even if it finds no breach of Article 8 in this case, the Court reiterates that this area needs to be kept under review by Contracting States' (quoted by Burns, 1998). In 2002 the case of Goodwin & I v. United Kingdom Government was a landmark case that set the GRA in motion. The ECHR held that the UK government's failure to alter the birth certificates of transsexual people and to allow them to marry in their new gender role was a breach of the European Convention on Human Rights. Following the decision Stephen Whittle from transgender political lobbying group 'PfC stated:

> Currently the government appears to be ignoring the decision, but there is good reason to think that English courts if asked to address any question of legal status, recognition or marriage, will interpret English law to follow the ECHR's [European Court of Human Rights] decision. Consequently we are encouraging everyone to go ahead now, and take advantage of the wonderful ECHR court victory by claiming their rights. The government needs to change the law in order to clarify it.
>
> Whittle (2002)

The significance of the three cases outlined lies in the challenges brought through human rights discourse and law to a biological model, which presumes a fixed relationship between 'sex' and gender identity. Legal challenges from UK citizens to this model are not new; in 1970, for example, the Corbett v. Corbett case received much publicity as it was heard in the UK courts. Arthur Corbett filed for divorce against the wishes of his wife April Corbett (formerly Ashley). The judge ruled, however, that since April had been born male, the marriage was never legal. This case set the precedent for several UK rulings that failed to recognise both gender reassignment and the partnerships of transgendered people. However, while the rulings in the UK courts were unequivocal about the connective relationship between 'sex' and gender, the judgements from the ECHR showed an awareness of the nuances of gender identity and practice, and the flexibility of family formations – even in the pre-Goodwin cases that ruled against the claimants. Specifically, the ECHR demonstrated an understanding of lived gender identities and experiences that are distinct from those defined at birth and of the need for state recognition of these identity practices. Thus European universal human rights discourse has often had an advantage over state law in its more flexible reading of gender and of gendered intimate relationships. However, as following chapters explore, because of the universality of human rights, these more progressive understandings are often diluted as human rights discourses become translated into state law. This is especially important as rights discourse is increasingly extended internationally and across cultural spheres.

Problematising the universalism of human rights

Chapter 1 addressed how human – or universal – rights are essential to much recognition theory, and particularly to the work of Charles Taylor. As Chapter 1 outlined, Taylor's (1995) theory of recognition distinguishes between a 'politics of difference' and a 'politics of universalism'. To recollect, a politics of difference stresses the importance of protecting individual or group identity and will be considered in depth in Chapter 7. According to Taylor, a politics of universalism relates to the 'equal dignity of all citizens' (1995: 233). All citizens, then, should be treated equally and all with respect – a sentiment apparent in the preamble to the UDHR adopted in 1948 by the United Nations: '[...] recognition of the inherent dignity and of the equality and unalienable right of all members of the human family is the foundation of freedom, justice and peace in the world'. Similar sentiments of universalism are apparent in Honneth's normative model of recognition, whereby, as discussed in Chapter 1, recognition is granted primordial significance.

Yet challenges to human rights discourse have long been levelled by feminists who have questioned the universal premise on which the human rights movement is based. A feminist critique of human rights (Pateman, 1989; Walby, 1994; Lister, 1997; Bussemaker and Voet, 1998; Okin, 1998; Daly and Cowen, 2000) points to the ways in which the rights of women have been marginalised through a continued focus on the 'rights of man' (Paine, 1792). Susan Okin (1998), for example, has highlighted the ways in which human rights documents have declared the rights of women without recognising that these rights may be different from the rights of men. A 'gender blind' model of human rights, Okin argues, arises since 'both the early conception of "the rights of man" in the 17th century and the original conception of international "human rights" in the 20th century were formulated with male family heads in mind' (1998:1). For these reasons, Wendy Brown believes that the value of rights language for women are 'paradoxes' – those that 'we cannot win' (Brown, 2000: 231).

Feminist scholars have also argued that human rights discourse fails to recognise diversities among the category of 'woman'. From this perspective, human rights discourse has protected the rights of middle-class, heterosexual, white western women at the expense of women whose cultural and social positionings lay outside these privileged frameworks. This critique is particularly evident in relation to how a universal human rights discourse around gender has neglected the particularities of race and ethnicity (Lewis, 1998). Gender theory has also critiqued a universal gendered model of citizenship for neglecting non-binary genders (Monro, 2005; Hines, 2006, 2007a). A gender binary model has discriminated against gender diverse people in terms of the redistributive (employment and welfare rights) and issues of recognition (the rights of self-identification in gender of choice). Challenges to a discourse of human rights from feminism and gender theory indicate the ways in which a discourse of human rights may protect the rights of the dominant over the marginal and, moreover, work to privilege certain social and cultural categories over others. Further, the discourse of universalism can actively construct experiences of exclusion. This point can be developed by examining sexuality studies' literature.

Critical readings of rights discourse from sexuality studies show the ways in which understandings and practices of sexuality are constructed. Scholars such as Carl Stychin (1998), Diane Richardson (1998), David Bell and Jon Binnie (2000) and Shane Phelan (2001), for example, articulate the ways in which rights discourses are constructed along a heterosexual model. Richardson argues that the granting of lesbian and gay rights leads to the privatisation and circumscription of these sexual identities: 'Lesbians and gay men are granted the right to be tolerated as long as they stay within the boundaries of that tolerance [...]' (1998: 90). This literature importantly indicates how a liberal human rights discourse privileges the rights of individuals and social groups who are able and/or willing to conform to normative ways of being. Moreover, these arguments shed light on how liberal universalism glosses over the ways in which the desire for rights is complexly situated.

Lois McNay (2008) develops an important critique of the role of universalism in recognition theory. Drawing on Foucault, McNay suggests that the drive towards recognition could be read as a symptom of increasing governmentality:

> For Foucault, for example, the pervasive desire for recognition would be a manifestation of an encroaching governmental power that controls individuals by manipulating the type of relation they have with themselves. The inculcation in individuals of a preoccupation with the self is not only compatible with an individualized consumerism, but also diffuses energies that might otherwise be directed towards more radical forms of social transformation. From a Foucauldian perspective, the quest for recognition shares the same structure as the confessional – the paradigm of disciplinary power – where individuals seek self – legitimation through being acknowledged within the normalising discourses of authority.
>
> McNay (2008: 133)

From a Foucauldian perspective, then, universal human rights can be read as the global intensification of governmentality. McNay also takes to task Honneth's view, as discussed in Chapter 1, that legal forms of recognition evidence moral progress, arguing that his 'naive' view fails to take account of the ways in which the law may also foreclose transformation – an argument, which will be evidenced in subsequent chapters in relation to the UK GRA.

Global misrecognition

A further, and highly significant, problem with universal models of recognition is the assumption that values and meaning easily travel from the West. In contrast, recent empirical research into sexuality at a European level (for example, by Binnie and Klesse, 2011; Kulpa and Mizielińska, 2012; Santos, 2013) points to the ways in which political models of sexual rights, equality and equal opportunity are frequently fixed to Western understandings of social justice. Such ways of understanding identity and politics at both subjective and structural levels are often very different in national contexts. From this insight, recognition theory and, particularly, its notions of universal rights can be seen to operate as a colonialising mechanism. Further, universal human rights may be viewed from this lens as a practice of neocolonial hegemony.

Scott Long (2009), Director of the LGBT Programme for Human Rights Watch New York, United States, raises similar points in his critique of the ways in which Western sexuality campaigners have (mis)read sexuality in Iran. In 2007, the Iranian state executed 21-year-old Makwan Mouloudzadeh – for alleged involvement in a rape when he was 13 years old. As Long notes, though Iran has one of the world's worst records on executions, most are deemed un-newsworthy. The case of Makwan Mouloudzadeh was different due to the reaction of sexual rights movements in the West. Mouloudzadeh had been convicted of raping three boys, even though the boys had later withdrawn their accusations and said that they had been made under duress. Long states that 'Makwan was not gay' (2009: 120) and, indeed, he was not accused of being gay. However, sexual rights movements in West vigorously argued that his execution was proof of a new Iranian policy to execute homosexuals. Neither of these claims could be evidenced (Long, 2009). Yet:

> The temptation to attribute 'gay' identity to Makwan was too great for many Western gays to pass up. An Amnesty International action stating that 'child offender Makwan Moloudzadeh' faced death for 'the alleged rape of a 13 year old boy' became in a US gay news site's headline 'Death penalty imminent for gay youth in Iran' (Towleroad, 2007). [...] Gay activists' conduct in the Makwan case was grounded in the politics of a country a continent away from Iran.
>
> Long (2009: 122)

In Long's discussion of the case, Peter Tatchell, UK gay rights campaigner and founder of *Outrage!*, was instrumental to this conduct.

Long details numerous responses from Tatchell and *Outrage!*, including the statement: 'This is just the latest barbarity by the Islamo-fascists in Iran (2009: 124)'. The story was then picked up by US gay commentator Andrew O'Sullivan who relayed it as a case of 'Islamists versus gays (2005)'. Further, O'Sullivan stated: 'I'm saddened that more gay organisations haven't rallied to the war against Muslim religious fanatics. This is our war too (2005)'. The sentiment "This is our war too" explicitly divides 'gay organisations' and 'Muslim's' foreclosing the possibility that one could be both. O'Sullivan's rallying cry to gays to join the war again Islam is echoed by Bruce Bawer's warning that 'European civilization is about to be overwhelmed by a flood of Muslim immigrants who will drown its institutions in fanaticism, its identity in sharia and its homosexuals in blood' (Bawer, 2006, cited in Long, 2009: 131).

For Long, the Makwan Mouloudzadeh case not only illustrates how the universalism of identity politics may lead to serious instances of misrecognition, but it also shows how emotions of recognition can be constructed with very problematic consequences. Thus disregarding the complexities of the case, 'our' sympathy is constructed for Makwan the gay youth killed by a fascist regime: 'sympathy depended on identity' (Long, 2009: 125). Further, the alleged victim of the case, another 13-year-old boy, does not receive sympathy at all: 'the limits of caring were being drawn' (Long, 2009: 125). These points resonate with Fraser's (2008) concern that a politics of recognition does not just reflect group differences, but may actually constitute difference and, thus, reinforce, conflict between groups, 'fuelling the very antagonisms one intended to regulate' (Fraser, 2008: 87).

The work of Jin Haritaworn, Tamsila Tauqir and Esra Erdemand is also important here in exploring how discourses of 'exceptionalism' (the belief that the West is at the forefront of sexual progress) reinforce the 'East' as a site of homophobia, which is then recolonised by 'the liberated West' (Haritaworn et al., 2008: 73). Within these practices of 'gay imperialism' (Haritaworn et al., 2008), recognition of the Muslim subject (as female, gay or lesbian) is as victim in need of liberation through Western models of recognition:

> In the current context of Islamophobia, white people are once again able to identify themselves as the global champions of 'civilisation', 'modernity' and 'development'. Gay Muslims are the latest symbol of this identity. They are the ideological token victim who

> must be liberated from its 'barbaric, backward' society, by means that include political and military violence. In this, Muslim gays are joining Muslim women, whose 'liberation', as postcolonial feminists have long argued, has traditionally provided the justification for imperialism.
>
> Haritaworn et al. (2008: 78)

Haritaworn et al. look to debates in Germany surrounding the 'Muslim Test' in 2006. Developed for migrants from 'Muslim' states, the first draft of the 'test' (which was later rejected due to the controversy it generated) asked questions largely based on attitudes towards terrorism, women and sexuality. Thus positive attitudes towards women and homosexuals were held as criteria by which migrants passed the test. As the authors state:

> This reflects a transformation of 'European' identities, which besides 'democracy' now claim 'women's equality' and 'gay rights' as symbols of their superior 'modernity' and 'civilisation'. This elevates gender and sexuality to mainstream political status. While we welcome this development, we find it vital to note that its main basis is not a progress in gender and sexual politics but a regression in racial politics.
>
> Haritaworn et al. (2008: 79)

Moreover, in contrast, the countries of immigration appear devoid of discrimination (2008: 83). Jasbir Puar's (2007) work offers a similar trenchant critique. Puar explores how neo-liberalism acts to incorporate *some* queer subjects into the nation state through recognition politics at the expense of others. In Puar's term, 'homonationalisms' are utilised in ways which divide the 'civilised' US citizen from the 'others'. This marker is no longer, she argues, one that necessarily links to a hetero/homo binary. Rather, the 'proper' US citizen may be heterosexual or homosexual, but the 'other' – the non-Western, the non-civilised – are likely to be 'racialized terrorist look-a-likes – especially Sikhs, Muslims, and Arabs – who are cordoned off for detention and deportation' (Puar, 2007: xxvii). Puar argues that the mainstreaming of certain queer subjects (notably, male, white and middle class) is in stark contrast to the exclusion of others. Further, the divide is at its starkest along the lines of race:

4 Claiming and Contesting Recognition

Introduction

While Chapter 1 empirically examined the meanings of recognition in considering how the term 'recognition' was understood by research participants, this chapter draws on empirical data to explore the significance of the 2004 UK GRA (GRA, 2004) for research participants as it came into law. By drawing on empirical data, the chapter examines the impact of recent policy and law on practices of gendered diversity as they are lived out in the everyday.

The chapter first considers the narratives of participants who have successfully registered for a GRC under the Act. Here I reflect on the practical benefits for trans people brought by the new framework of rights. The chapter then turns to the narratives of participants who were not able to, or chose not to, register for gender recognition. Debates around recognition will be considered alongside a rejection of authenticity and assimilation, wherein recognition is subject to dissent at both subjective and conceptual levels. Questions about the value of recognition for gender and sexual politics will be raised by empirically examining the social and cultural consequences for those who cannot, or will not, seek 'gender recognition'.

The pragmatics of recognition

My research indicates that many trans people feel that they have benefitted to some degree from the new rights brought by the GRA. As discussed in Chapter 1, for many participants an identity politics of esteem and autonomy is evident when considering the meanings of recognition. The empirical material from Chapter 1 illustrated the ways in which participants often spoke about recognition as inferring increased societal acceptance, understanding and legitimacy of gender diversity. Importantly, though, in reflecting on the *significance* of the GRA – *why* they saw it as important, *why* they wished to register – in the main, strategic, rather than symbolic, reasons were articulated. Such ambiguities and levels of pragmatism are reflected in Tasha's biography. In 2004, Tasha had gender reassignment surgery and in 2006 successfully applied under the GRA for gender recognition. Tasha fulfilled the criteria for gender recognition and was able to provide the Gender Recognition Panel with the required evidence. Yet the ways in which Tasha discusses her gender identity are far from straightforward; as the following interview extract illustrates:

> Interviewer: Could you tell me a little about your gender identity?
>
> Tasha: Depends on the mood. I don't like being classified. For the GRC I'm a lot happier being classified as female than I am being classified as male. I certainly don't want to be classified as male, but I feel that I have some male characteristics, so in-between that's where I see myself. But if someone can't get his head round that then I'm female (Tasha, age 52)

Far from articulating an inherent gender identity, Tasha discusses the variability of gender expression. Further, she rejects binary gender classification, instead presenting gender as a spectrum. While she suggests that she identifies more as female than male, she does not rule out elements of masculinity. Such complexities of gender identification and expression, however, go unrecognised in the GRA, which, as the next section of the chapter examines, demands that participants such as Tasha select a gender of male or female for official classification. Tasha presents an account that separates her official classification from her other gendered 'moods', demonstrating reflective awareness of legal restraints. In considering the significance of the GRA, Tasha focuses upon the practical benefits of state recognition:

> Some things do feel nice. The driving licence form: 'use this form to announce a change of address, name or sex'; great! I remember

> that because that pleased me. Yes, it lightens the load doesn't it? I think yes, it lightens the load. It is on the whole better that the state thinks of me as a female.
>
> (Tasha, age 52)

For Tasha, a GRC makes life smother on a practical level. In using the phrase 'on the whole', though, she offers a somewhat reluctant attitude to the significance of recognition. What largely matters to Tasha, as to other participants who have registered, or wish to register, under the GRA, are the practical legal benefits. Like Tasha, Nick distanced subjective gender identity from the legal significance of recognition:

> For me it is more of a convenience thing I don't think it will affect me in terms of my identity [...] I don't feel in any shape or form that I need a passport or a birth certificate to feel more strongly towards my identity I just need it for practical reasons.
>
> (Nick, age 30)

The symbolic importance of state recognition of gender is complexly related and most participants were ambivalent, rather than affirmative, about the importance of legal recognition as 'male' or 'female'. This is further apparent in Tasha's narrative when she considers binary legal understandings of gender as either/or (male/female):

> Let's see; the state says I am a man – definite no-no. I don't like that at all. The state says I am a woman... I'm much keener on that but it's not perfect... What I would want is that the state admits that my retirement age is 60 whatever gender I am and that the state has no interest at all what sex I am.
>
> (Tasha, age 52)

Yet, as the next section of the chapter explores, the GRA indicates the extent to which the state maintains a preoccupation with gender orientation.

Conceptual shifts and medical hangovers

As I suggested in Chapter 1, the GRA recognises gender as separate from 'sex' as defined at birth and brings a new framework of rights, which acknowledge that gender may change across the life course. Such acknowledgement, however, is partial and, moreover, remains tied to medical discourse and practice. Applications for recognition under the GRA are made to the Ministry of Justice and are considered individually by a Gender Recognition Panel, which consists of judicially trained legal and medical members who assess the documentation provided in the application. First, the evidence required for recognition demands that an applicant 'has lived in the acquired gender throughout the period of two years ending with the date on which the application is made' and 'intends to continue to live in the acquired gender until death' (GRA, 2004). Thus those who do not firmly and permanently identify as male or as female remain misrecognised in law as the complexities of their gendered subjectivities go unaccounted for. Second, determination of applications is based on the Gender Recognition Panel being satisfied that the applicant: 'has or has had gender dysphoria' (GRA, 2004). The concept of 'gender dysphoria' has long been central to medical understandings of transsexualism. Locked into the notion of 'gender dysphoria' is the idea of the 'wrong body', which suggests transsexualism is a biological state of discord between 'sex' (the body) and gender identity (the mind) (Hines, 2007a). The concept of 'gender dysphoria' remains a key classificatory term within medical discourse and practice. Further, 'gender dysphoria' is read as symptomatic of 'gender identity disorder', which is currently a category listed in the *Diagnostic and Statistical Manual of Mental Disorders* (*DSM*), a handbook for mental health professionals on diagnosing mental illnesses. Thus the continued influence of medical understandings and the persistent role of the medical practitioner in enabling – or disabling – recognition are starkly evident.

Grounds of evidence prove complex and my research findings indicate that applications that were rejected were done so on the grounds of a lack of medical evidence. Several participants spoke of finding the gender recognition process complicated and frustrating. Some participants had their evidence questioned and others had it disputed; Susan's narrative offers an example:

> The major bugbear of mine is providing the diagnosis report. It's a nightmare. I had to be re-diagnosed. Right, I was diagnosed years ago... why do I have to be re-diagnosed? It's crazy. I came across a

> sticking point [...] Even though I've been through surgery, even though I've changed my name for six years, it's perfectly clear what I've done. Which is really stupid, so I asked my GP to check their records and they found an initial diagnosis from X in 2001 and that initial diagnosis did say I had gender dysphoria, which is exactly what the GRP forms requested. I sent a letter back saying 'that's it, that's all I can find you, like it or lump it,' and finally that's been enough.
>
> (Susan, age 42)

Knowledge of such complications among trans communities meant that other participants did not begin the application process as they felt unsure of the status of their evidence.

These issues led some participants to speak out against the medical evidence that was required by the Gender Recognition Panel, with issues of privacy and potential disclosure of trans status being cited as particularly problematic areas. Heather, for example, refused to supply the required evidence, believing that it broke ethics of confidentiality:

> I felt that the Gender Recognition Act was asking for a level of personal disclosure that was a breach of your medical confidentiality; in terms of the medical evidence that they were requiring [...] Because these are highly personal issues, you know, when you go into a counselling session with a gender therapist and you're talking about things to do with your family life, your love life, your sex life, how you felt as a child [...] And I thought, 'no', that's just wrong, that's inherently wrong. And I thought, OK, I object to that... I think this is a breach of medical confidentiality and I thought I'm not willing to do that.
>
> (Heather, age 39)

Further, transitioning outside the medical system leaves one without the diagnosis of 'gender dysphoria' that is needed for a successful application, as Karen's narrative reflects:

> I have been trying to get a sex change since October 26th of 2004 when I first went to the doctors. And here we are four and half years later no further forward basically except in that

> time I must have had about nine or ten assessments by different psychiatrists.
>
> (Karen, age 61)

The key role occupied by medical practitioners and, particularly, psychiatrists in the recognition process was frequently articulated as producing a convoluted experience. When asked about how easy he found the gender recognition process, Andrew, for example, said:

> I've contacted the gender clinic for letters for my application but they have not got back in touch with me and I don't even know if my letters have even reached the right people. I sent it to the right place but whether it has been passed from secretary to the psychiatrist I don't know. I can't possibly know that. So I don't know if things have gone missing or if it is in a pile of somebody's inbox somewhere with a load of other stuff or if it even arrived in the first place [...] I don't even see why you need psychiatrist evidence.
>
> (Andrew, age 30)

The involvement of psychiatrists in the legal process was a source of discontent for many participants. Reflecting this, Fiona stated:

> No psychiatrists should be involved. This is not a mental illness. And in other parts of the world they're enlightened enough not to use mental health professionals any more. [...] It is absolutely appalling. It is the biggest affront to human rights as far as transgender and transsexual people, because both are tarred with the same brush. It is the fundamental issue. We have to remove this.
>
> (Fiona, age 58)

Here Fiona refers to the differences between transsexual and transgender people – between people who firmly articulate a gender identity that is the opposite of that which was defined at birth and those for whom gender identification lies between or beyond the binary of male and female. The specificities of each group, Fiona believes, are not addressed in law. Some participants believed that the guiding framework of gender recognition should be separated altogether from a biological model of 'sex' and gender:

> Western society is obsessed with gender and sex. The law should be framed in human rights terms, rather than in a binary notion of gender.
>
> (Jude, age 45)

The majority of participants felt that the GRC discriminated against people whose identity was not straightforwardly male or female. Many participants did say that they broadly identified as either male or female and so were not personally affected by having to identify in this way in order to register for recognition. Most of these participants, however, felt that the Act was unfair for those whose gender identities were not binary; as Jude reflects: 'If people are happy to be not either man or woman, if that is how they perceive themselves to be, then that should be recognised' (Jude, age 45). Several participants felt that in order to obtain a GRC, they had to fit into the categories of male and female when their gender identity was more complex, as indicated by Jan: 'When you have to tick the boxes on a form I would usually put my tick in the middle' (Jan, age 51).

Transgender campaigning groups fought hard for the GRA to have non-surgical criteria of recognition, and, subsequently, surgery is not required for gender recognition. All but one of the participants felt that it was positive that the criteria did not involve surgery. It was felt that surgical criteria would have been discriminatory on a number of levels: against people who could not afford private surgery and were on the Nationa Health Service (NHS) waiting lists, against people who were unable to have surgery due to medical reasons and for people who chose not to have surgery.

Despite the non-surgical criteria, however, the GRA was criticised by participants for its failure to offer recognition for people who did not identify as male or as female; all but one of the participants argued that the GRA discriminated against people whose identity was not straightforwardly male or female. Cheryl, for example, said:

> It's dividing the world into good trannies and bad trannies. And ok, I happen to be lucky that I fall into the good trannie mould but I have many friends who don't and I think the world should be nice to them as well as being nice to me.
>
> (Cheryl, age 51)

While Cheryl talks of her solidarity with trans people whose gender identities are more fluid than hers – relating to constructions of good/bad citizen that will be picked up in Chapter 5 – several participants felt that in order to obtain a GRC, they themselves had to comply with categories of male or female even though their gender identity was more complex. From this juncture, some activists are currently arguing for the legal framework of the GRA to be expanded. Central issues here are the extension of recognition to non-gendered people and removing the requirement for medical evidence. For other participants, though, the concept of recognition remains unintelligible, leading to their rejection of state recognition.

Rejecting recognition

For those whose gender identity and presentation falls between or outside the binary of male/female, both the notion and process of recognition prove impenetrable. Research participant Christie, for example, identifies as 'non-gendered'. Christie's rejection of a gender binary means that Christie is denied the rights afforded by the GRA. Thus, for Christie: 'The GRA has made no positive impact on my life...' (Christie). Christie continued:

> Many transpeople, including some transsexuals, do not meet the criteria to have their birth certificate amended under the statutory terms of the GRA. The GRA opens up citizenship rights for transsexuals who can tick all the right boxes [...] The GRA does not benefit any 'transgendered' individual who does not identify as either 100 per cent male or 100 per cent female, or anyone who is transsexual but, for whatever reason, does not live full time within their chosen gendered role.
>
> (Christie)

Christie's narrative sheds light on the ways in which a binary gender model works to construct a divide between trans people. Such considerations resonate with the arguments of critical sexual citizenship scholars, which, as Chapter 6 explores, point to the ways in which a neoliberal agenda around sexuality pits the 'good gay' against the 'bad queer' (Stychin, 1998). Correspondingly, the 'good' trans subject occupies a full-time and permanent male or female gender identity, while the 'bad' trans person refuses to choose. Paradoxically, then, gendered *non-recognition* emerged as a key research theme. Jasmine, for example, said:

> You know, if gender was a lot more fluid we wouldn't have to worry about it and the whole legal thing wouldn't be an issue. I mean, I suppose it makes me angry that we have to have a GRA at all [...] And another thing that makes me angry about the GRA is how narrow their definition of being trans is and how exclusive it is.
>
> (Jasmine, age 36)

Jasmine points to the ways in which the legal imaginary fails to comprehend the complexities of lived experience. Foreclosure of the recognition of gender identities and expressions that are not male or female thus constructs, as Jasmine indicates, a 'narrow' gendered schema. Jasmine's 'anger' is politicised by other research participants, for whom 'recognition' is problematically linked to assimilation. In this way, Joe connects his decision not to register for gender recognition to a refusal to assimilate:

> Hanging on to my female birth certificate is fine. I actually want to do that. I just don't see the point [in registering for a Gender Recognition Certificate]. I've decided to be quite out about being trans. And that's a political thing.
>
> (Joe, age 50)

Such levels of individual defiance, I suggest, are reflective of a broader politics of resistance, which problematise and stand against a neoliberal perspective on 'equality and diversity'. The narratives of research participants who chose not to register for a GRC can thus be read as offering a politics of non-recognition, which, in turn, links with broader radical gender and sexual movements that are organising against both the concept and the implementation of 'equality'. Joe, for example, discussed his decision not to seek gender recognition as one which was politically guided:

> There's also a political side for me as well that thinks why do we have to go through that process? I don't see why a panel of

> non-trans people has to make a decision on whether I'm trans or not. And this whole thing of having to prove your diagnosis either to doctors or to ... you know I just think that's a load of crap. What does it have to do with them? I don't need to prove myself to anybody. And what harm does it do to anybody else, that this is who I am? So I don't want to go through that process. And lots of people can't.
>
> (Joe, age 50)

In rejecting recognition, Joe forges alliances with trans people who are marginalised by the evidence-based criteria of recognition and offers a strong critique of the medicalisation of transgender. In choosing not to register for gender recognition, the notion of gender itself is problematised, and medical knowledge and authority challenged. A politics of non-recognition thus points to both the personal and the political comprises inherent in a politics of gender recognition. It rejects the notion of the stable gendered subject and foregrounds the experience of gender diversity and, accordingly, contests the central tenets of identity politics.

Contesting identity politics

In discussing recognition theory, Chapter 1 addressed how identity has been theorised as central to recognition politics. Though from different perspectives, each of the writers from the recognition literature considered in Chapter 1 foreground shared identity as a prerequisite for recognition: thus common experiences of inequality are collectively articulated, acting as the precursor for the development of rights-based politics. In tracing rights-based politics of gender and sexual movements, Chapter 2 also addressed how understandings and practices of belonging developed from collective experiences – and the sharing of such experiences – of inequality. Yet in discussing gender diversity, Chapter 2 additionally considered how a politics of belonging (of some) may also work to exclude (others); hence the chapter explored how trans people were alienated from both feminist and sexual movements. A politics of identity is therefore nebulous and, I would suggest, untenable as a principle for social justice.

A critique of identity politics underscored the development of queer theory and politics in the 1990s. Queer scholars and activists have thus emphasised the ways in which identity politics derive from a hetero/homo binary that fails to acknowledge the diversity of sexual desires, behaviours, identities and politics. Similarly, as Chapter 2 illustrated, and as I have written about elsewhere (Hines, 2005, 2007a, 2010), the identity of 'woman' that drove feminist politics has worked against both trans men and women. Though identity politics has largely been theorised as a vital step to social justice within the recognition literature, there have been notes of caution in this body of work too. Reflecting this, Nancy Fraser argues:

> The identity model politics of recognition tends to reify group identities. Stressing the need to elaborate and display an authentic, self-affirming, and self-generated collective identity, it puts moral pressure on individual members to conform to group culture. Cultural dissidence and experimentation are accordingly discouraged, when they are not simply equated with disloyalty. So, too, is cultural criticism, including efforts to explore intra-group divisions, such as those of gender, sexuality and class. [...] The overall effect is to impose a single, drastically simplified group identity which denies the complexity of people's lives, the multiplicity of their identifications, and the cross-pulls of their various affiliations.
>
> Fraser (2003: 26)

Fraser's arguments here speak not only to divisions within feminist and sexual rights communities, as indicated above, but also to fractures within trans communities. The issue of identity politics as an excluding mechanism, for example, is apparent in my earlier research on transgender practices of identity (Hines, 2007a). Here, research findings indicated that assertions of authenticity and gendered 'realness' within some trans communities served to exclude people who were not considered to be 'genuine' – largely people who were not embarking on the medical route to gender transition (see also Davy, 2011). The effects of such battles of authenticity serve to rupture an already fragile community. As Fraser continues:

> Ironically, then, the identity model serves as a vehicle of misrecognition. In reifying group identity, finally, it obscures the politics of cultural identification, the struggles *within* the group or the authority, and indeed the power, to represent it. By shielding

> such struggles from view, it tends to mask the power of dominant factions and thus to reinforce intragroup domination. Thus, the identity model lends itself all too easily to repressive forms of communitarianism, which promote conformism, intolerance, and patriarchalism.
>
> Fraser (2003: 26)

Fraser's sentiments here are important. My empirical research on transgender practices of identity indicated deep struggles around the authentic trans experience, demonstrations of which marginalised the most vulnerable within trans communities (Hines, 2007a). Fraser's notion of 'misrecognition' aptly delineates power struggles within social movements as well as speaking to the lack of value attributed to marginal identities by dominant culture. Yet, such internal struggles are also sustained by dominant external systems. Hence the GRA affords rights to some trans people while further marginalising others (Hines, 2010). As Wendy Brown argues, discourse of identity and recognition may translate into a 'language of unfreedom' (1995: 66). Similarly, in her consideration of same sex spousal equality (arguments around which will be developed in Chapter 5), Davina Cooper evaluates the extent to which 'struggles to undercut one form of inequality may work to reinforce others' (Cooper, 2004: 114). For Cooper, this is dependent upon the extent to which legal reform leads to a reordering of normative principles, the latter which 'secure and strengthen dominant social relations largely through the ways in which they protect the status quo' (Cooper, 2004: 114). As she argues, normative principles are no more static than is the law, since normative principles are subject to change, and face ongoing confrontation from oppositional or counter-normative articulations' (Cooper, 2004: 114). However, as Cooper acknowledges, *some* changes for *some* groups may be more in reach than others.

In their discussion of recognition politics, McLaughlin, Phillimore and Richardson pose the following question: 'Do we live in a moment where recognition is opening up to allow for greater space for varied or hybrid forms of living and mutual valuation, provided with rights and protection? Or is recognition paradoxically a means to narrow down options to more restrictive categories of acceptable ways of living and legitimate access to rights?' (2001: 2). This question is at the core of the tensions around recognition that have been discussed in this chapter and, on a first reading, the former seems to be affirmed. Ironically, then, the GRA can be seen to close down both understandings and practices of gender diversity, as it produces the gender binary system anew.

Nevertheless, as the narratives of research participants considered above infer, a more optimistic picture can also be drawn. As illustrated above, Joe, for instance, positioned his refusal of recognition relationally: 'And lots of people can't' (Joe, age 50). Moreover, as discussed in this chapter, the vast majority of research participants were critical of the GRA for not representing trans people whose gender did not fit a binary model of male/female, regardless of their own gender identity. Therefore, constraints on gendered freedoms emerging from legal frameworks can be seen to enable new practices of resistance and unchartered alliances within communities.

Conclusion

This chapter has empirically explored the successes of recognition claims for those who wish to seek 'gender recognition'. Research findings indicate that the GRA has had positive impacts for many participants in terms of the practical benefits it has brought in enabling trans people to change their birth certificates and other key documents. For some participants, the GRA also brought increased esteem through the legitimation of their identity. In these ways, the Act may be theorised as indicating the successes of a politics of recognition.

Yet the participants' narratives discussed in this chapter also tell a more complex story. While many participants spoke pragmatically about the benefits of the GRA, they also refuted the impact upon on their sense of self – upon their gendered subjectivity. Thus, while participants often welcomed the ways the GRA had made their lives smoother on a practical level, most did not feel that it had strengthened their self-identity. Moreover, some participants felt that the Act had further marginalised their position in society and spoke of the fragmentation this had brought on a psycho-social level. For people who had not followed a medically approved route to gender transition and/or did not identify as male or female, then, the GRA had detrimental effects which yielded new patterns of misrecognition and marginalisation.

In his discussion of politics of cultural recognition, Kwame Appiah (1994) relates the contradictions apparent here. Stories of shared identity, he suggests, are important to self-understanding and belonging, yet they can also close down individual creativity – the ability to produce one's own story. In this way, my research findings indicate that individual practices of gender diversity go unrecognised in the legal framework that the GRA has generated. While the law now recognises that gendered identification may change, only a particular path of gender change is granted recognition. However, rather than crushing individual or collective creativity, research narratives indicate resistance at both individual and collective levels. Lack of provision for non-gendered people and for people who have transitioned outside the medical system has thus led to practices of non-recognition, which challenge voices of authority and certification. As Chapter 5 will explore, very similar debates emerge when considering the ways in which the GRA speaks to practices of intimacy and to personal lives.

5
Recognising and Regulating Intimate Diversity

Introduction

This chapter broadens out from the concerns around self or group identity that have been addressed in the previous chapters to look at rights-based claims by gender and sexual movements that have addressed areas of intimate life. Here the chapter draws on sociological arguments concerning the diversity of intimate practices and affective ties in contemporary society. It considers Axel Honneth's (1995) notion of love as a site of recognition in reflecting on the claims for intimate recognition made by gender and sexuality-based movements.

The chapter addresses how the UK 2004 CPA was developed in tandem to the GRA, looking at connections across these laws and assessing the ways in which each law was developed with the other in mind. It then moves on to examine recent campaigns for, and debates around, equal marriage within sexual rights movements. Later sections of the chapter empirically explore the impact of the GRA on affective ties and intimate relationships. It first considers the narratives of participants who suggest that the Act has had a positive effect on these areas of their lives and moves on to look at participants' narratives that point to greater constraint in personal lives as a result of legal change. Notions of recognition are addressed alongside critical debates around assimilationism. Here I draw on a range of different approaches to intimate life from scholars and sexual movement activists. These positions, I suggest, run counter to a politics of equality, offering, instead, a politics of 'non-recognition'.

Sociologies of intimacy

Sociological work has widely suggested that intimacy has become a site of social transformation within modern society. In the work of Anthony Giddens (1992) and Ulrich Beck and Elisabeth Beck-Gernsheim (1995), intimacy acquires new meanings and an increased importance in contemporary society. For Giddens an 'ideal of intimacy' (1992) is personified by the desire for a 'pure' relationship, which represents greater levels of emotional and sexual democracy, with the stress on choice and trust. An important feature of the pure relationship arises from 'plastic sexuality' (Giddens, 1992), where sexuality attains distinct signification as it becomes liberated from reproduction. Although Giddens sees such shifts as taking place within heterosexual relationships, he suggests that lesbians and gay men have long been practitioners of the pure relationship in which notions of equality and autonomy are held central. While Lynne Jamieson (1998) warns against overstating the extent of the pure relationship in stressing how structural inequalities continue to hamper its existence, she too concedes that same-sex relationships offer its greatest potential. Likewise, Jackie Stacey positions lesbian and gay families as the 'pioneer outpost of the postmodern family condition, confronting most directly its features of improvisation, ambiguity, diversity, contradiction, self-reflection and flux' (Stacey, 1996: 142).

The empirical study carried out by Jeffery Weeks et al. (2001) also suggests that developments in non-heterosexual patterns of intimacy are linked to wider changes in society. They suggest that exploring the social organisation of what they term 'families of choice' enables a greater understanding of changes within the family and intimate relationships in general. Weeks et al. (2001) find a diversity of 'life experiments' underway, which supports Gillian Dunne's (1999) assertion that same-sex intimate and partnering relationships hold greater possibilities of equality in the organisation of domestic life, employment and childcare.

Central to the work on non-heterosexual patterns of partnering and parenting is the emphasis placed on emotional agency. Writing about lesbian and gay kinship networks, Jillian Sandell (1994) points to the queering of emotional boundaries within extended kinship patterns. She suggests that these affective relationships reflect fluidity in the demarcation of friends and lovers. This point has also been made by Weeks et al. (2001), Sasha Roseneil (2000) and Roseneil and Shelley Budgeon (2004). Additionally, the body of work on non-heterosexual relationships supports the assertion that individualisation and detraditionalisation within modern society have led to greater levels of reflexivity (Giddens, 1992; Castells, 1997; Weeks et al., 2001; Bauman, 2003). While the degree of individual and collective agency is undeniably uneven and subject to structural constraints (Skeggs, 1997, 2011; Jamieson, 1998; Lawler, 2005; Taylor, 2007, 2009, 2012; McDermott, 2011), there is considerable evidence of heightened degrees of agency in the creation of equitable and caring social networks within studies of non-heterosexual patterns of partnering and parenting. Moreover, the creative shifts in same-sex patterns of partnering, parenting and friendship can shed light upon the changing role of intimacy within wider society. Kath Weston's premise that gay kinship ideologies have 'transformed, rather than copied, existing kinship networks' (Weston cited in Sandell, 1994: 9) is relevant here, as is Roseneil's (2000) assertion that the heterosexual/homosexual binary is increasingly fragile within contemporary society. Likewise, Weeks et al. point to an 'increasing flexibility' and '"moral fluency" in intimate life, which stretches across the heterosexual-homosexual divide' (Weeks et al., 2001: 20).

While studies of same-sex intimacies pose a challenge to sociologies of the family, which have theorised intimacy through an all-exclusive focus upon the nuclear, heterosexual, monogamous, reproductive family, non-normative patterns of intimacy tend to still be relegated to 'subfields of the sociologies of family and gender' (Roseneil and Budgeon, 2004: 136). As Sandell (1994) argues, these developments hold political possibilities for alliances between a diversity of non-traditional family groupings. Yet, until recently (Hines, 2006a, 2006b, 2007a; Sanger, 2010), the intimate lives and affective networks of trans people were not accounted for in sociologies of intimacy, the family and personal life. Though the impact of gender transition upon intimate relationships and affective ties – with partners, lovers, children, friends, extended family members – will differ within individual circumstance, the process of transition will always also take place within a social framework (Hines, 2006a). A dialogical approach to intimacy allows us to broaden the analytical framework beyond one of individualism – or matters of 'choice' – to examine the ways in which patterns of intimacy are always tied to structural forces. This is not to deny agency, but rather to acknowledge how agentic processes are continuously negotiated alongside structural restraints. From this premise, the law can both enable and deter individual, collective and intimate processes of recognition.

Recognising love and intimacy

Axel Honneth's (1995) work on recognition identifies three modes of recognition: love, respect and esteem – the latter two modes which were discussed in Chapter 1. Love, Honneth suggests, characterises 'strong emotional attachment among a small number of people' (1995: 95), which defines 'primary affectional relationships' (1995: 1996). Honneth links these instances of love to that between romantic partners, parents and children and friends. Honneth prioritises love as a mode of recognition above respect and esteem due to his belief that love and bodily self-confidence are intertwined. As Simon Thompson explains: 'Only if I have self-confidence will I be able to acquire self-respect, where this means regarding myself as a rationally autonomous agent. And only if I have self-confidence will I be able to esteem myself, where this means believing that I make a valuable contribution to society' (2006: 26). For Honneth, then, recognition of love is the precedent of the other modes, as without the recognition of love, respect and esteem – both for one's self and for others – is not possible. Charles Taylor (1995) also addresses intimacy in theorising recognition although, unlike Honneth, he distinguishes the 'intimate sphere' from that of the 'public sphere'. Though most of Taylor's work focuses on the latter, his writing on intimacy binds relational ties to self-identity: 'On the intimate level, we can see how much an original identity needs and is vulnerable to the recognition given or withheld by significant others' (1995: 232).

The centralising of intimacy in a politics of recognition has been legislated for at the level of European Human Rights through *Article 8: the right to respect for private and family life, and Article 12: the right to marry and found a family* of the Human Rights Act (1998). As Chapter 3 addressed, it was *Article 8* and *Article 12* that were cited in the ECHR by trans people who argued that UK law prevented these rights. Chapter 3 also discussed the ways in which the ECHR was instrumental to the development of the UK GRA (2004). Thus the protection of intimate relationships was a keystone of legal moves to grant transgender people recognition. A GRC enables a person to change their birth certificate and then to marry someone of the opposite gender or to form a civil partnership with someone of the same gender. Some research participants had taken up these new rights and spoke positively about being able to formulise these relationships. Amanda, for example, said: 'The positives are obviously it's allowed me to get a birth certificate, obviously allowed me to get married, so that side of things is great' (Amanda, age 58). In these instances, the GRA has brought relationship recognition alongside gender recognition. Amelia drew on the significance of relationship recognition in saying: 'It meant I was able to enter into a civil partnership, you know, with all the fanfare that that takes, rather than having to hide away and pretend' (Amelia, age 46). Yet, as the next section of this chapter shows, for other people, the GRA has failed to provide protection for marriage and family life, and, moreover, has had the counter effect of disintegrating these areas of personal life.

The divorce clause

Participants largely felt that their relationships with family members and close friends had been unaffected by the GRA. Gender transition more broadly was discussed as the factor that strained or deepened familial and friendship bonds, and the GRA was not believed to have affected this either positively or negatively. Lucy reflected this in saying: 'My friends are my friends regardless and things with my family have not changed because of that' (Lucy, age 49). When asked about the impact of the GRA on intimate life, the 'divorce clause' was the point participants felt strongly about. If an applicant for gender recognition is not married, she/he will be granted a full GRC, which then allows for the change of birth certificate. If she/he is married, she/he receives an interim certificate, with the full certificate being granted when the marriage is annulled. The applicant has six months in which to divorce. For people who remained married to their pre-transition partners the legislation is deeply problematic. The dilemma faced by these applicants for gender recognition (and their partners) is whether to divorce in order to fulfil the criteria for recognition. Lucy talked about her own situation in this way:

> X [participant's wife] wanted to remain married [...] I feel that I have obligations to X. I mean our relationship is in some ways very similar to how it used to be, in terms of a responsibility relationship. And that is likely to continue because I take that responsibility seriously. [...] The continuation of that relationship has not enabled me to take some of the steps perhaps that I would have wanted to take to free myself from the past. I'm still fulfilling for X that role as husband; not sexually but in other ways. And I still fulfil the role for my children. And I don't want to take that away from them.
>
> (Lucy, age 49)

In defence of the divorce clause, Ministers had argued that following divorce and gender recognition, people would be able to register their marriage under the 2004 CPA. The GRA and the CPA, then, were developed in tandem and are co-positioned in practice. What this does not take account of, however, are the ways in which the intersections between gender and sexuality are multifarious (Hines, 2010) and the instances of intimacy that are practiced between and beyond the binaries of male/female, homo/hetero. Linking the GRA and the CPA carries a set of assumptions about gender and sexuality, and intimate life. First it assumes a hetero/homo binary; one can be heterosexual (marry) or homosexual (civilly partner). Second it assumes a connective relationship between gender and sexuality. Butler's (1990) notion of the 'heterosexual matrix' denotes the cultural framework of interpretation that makes sex, gender and desire intelligible. In this matrix, 'sex' denotes not only appropriate gender but also correct sexuality. The GRA and the CPA may have made room for genders and sexualities that operate outside the matrix; however, these identities are discursively constructed as, and restricted to, a binary either/or – male/female – homo/hetero. What is lost here are the ways in which gender identity and sexuality are complexly understood, experienced and practiced outside these epistemological binaries.

None of the participants in this research project felt that the CPA alleviated discrimination for trans people in existing marriages. Civil partnerships were not believed to be on an equal footing – either symbolically or legally – to marriage, and participants often said that linking the two pieces of legislation demonstrated a lack of understanding of the complexities between gender and sexuality. Thus Jo said:

> A civil partnership is not appropriate at all. It's inappropriate for trans people in lots of ways. A civil partnership is not equal to marriage. And it just doesn't... there's no logic to it. What's the logic? It's completely asymmetrical.
>
> (Jo, age 45)

Elsewhere (Hines, 2006, 2007a) I have suggested that incorporating transgender practices of partnering and parenting into sociologies of intimacy enables a richer understanding of the dynamics of contemporary 'life experiments' (Weeks et al., 2001). My broader research has shown that practices of intimacy within transgender partnering and parenting relationship are amenable to complex shifts in gendered and meaning and expression. The incorporation of transgender practices of intimacy into analyses of contemporary patterns of sociality thus sheds further light upon the ways in which intimate relationships are subject to ongoing contest, negotiation and innovation (Hines, 2006). However, my research on the GRA suggests that agentic intimate practices are hampered by current UK law. In this way, the GRA was strongly criticised by the majority of participants for its criteria that those married to their pre-transition partners divorce before being granted a GRC. Regardless of individual relationship status, or whether or not the divorce clause had a personal effect, the majority of participants spoke very strongly against this aspect of the law, describing it as 'outrageous', 'disgusting', 'unfair in the extreme'. Likewise, Tony said:

> This part of the legislation is a disgrace. Families are being torn apart. What about the supposed stress on 'family values'? So trans people's families clearly don't matter, don't measure up.
>
> (Tony, age 38)

Here Tony develops a strong political critique of government rhetoric around 'family values', pointing out how certain families are imbued with 'value' at the expense of others–in this case the families of trans people. As subsequent sections in this chapter consider, research findings point to two very different ways of responding to these inequalities: one is to campaign for equal marriage laws, the other is to refute marriage.

I do: From civil partnerships to equal marriage

The recognition of same-sex partnerships has long been central to rights-based political campaigns. Social movement demands for same-sex marriage in the United Kingdom led to the 2004 CPA, while in the United Kingdom, the United States and across Europe, same-sex marriage remains high on the political agenda. Campaigns for partnership recognition are based on demands for equality with heterosexual couples – the right to have relationships legitimised and the right to the same benefits, for example, next of kin rights, parenting rights, tax, inheritance and pension rights. The discourse of campaigns for same-sex partnership recognition echoes that of recognition politics and the claim for equality is based around the notion of 'sameness' – same-sex relationships are no less valuable than heterosexual partnerships and members should be treated equally. This argument fuelled the campaign for partnership recognition in the United Kingdom by 'Stonewall', the UKs largest Lesbian and Gay campaigning organisation. On the inception of the CPA, 'Stonewall' reiterated narratives of sameness in their partnership recognition literature. For example, *You're Gay, You're In Love, You Want to be Together Forever... Get Hitched!: A Guide to Civil Partnerships* states that the CPA is a 'path to equality, you get every right and every privilege – and every responsibility – straight couples get when they marry. It's the same thing. You can even ask your relations for toasters' (Stonewall, 2005). The publication goes on to stress that with every equal *right* comes equal *responsibility* – sentiments that sit tightly with a neo-liberal model of citizenship that will be explored in Chapter 6.

A normalising discourse can also be found among some gay writers, for example, Bruce Bawer (1994) claims that the lifestyles of gay people are indistinguishable from those of heterosexual couples, while Andrew Sullivan (1995) declares that gay people have the same values and aspirations as heterosexuals and simply seek integration into society. While writers such as Bawer and Sullivan represent the extreme of an assimilationist agenda that distances itself from 'unrelated revolutionary agendas' (Bawer, 1994) in a bid to be 'virtually normal' (Sullivan, 1995), a strand of sexual politics primarily concerned with rights-based claims has taken principal place within sexual social movements. Moreover, this agenda comes from factions that have entered mainstream political cultures with high degrees of cultural and material capital.

Subsequently, a number of writers have challenged a discourse of partnership 'equality'. David Evans (1993), Rosemary Hennessy (2000), Mandy Merk (2007) and Yvette Taylor (2007), among others, have written critically on the relationship between sexuality, subjectivity and the economy. These approaches dispute a functionalist position that suggests that capitalism requires that homosexuals occupy a subsidiary societal position, pointing instead to the cooption of 'lifestyle sexuality' by capitalist economies. Evans's *Sexual Citizenship: The Material Construction of Sexualities* (1993) offers an early analysis of the interrelationship between sexuality, the market and the state. Evans argues that the state capitalises on the economic power held by some sexual minority groups, for example, middle class gay men. While this citizen may hold economic rights, he nevertheless remains an 'immoral' citizen. Moreover, sexual minorities who hold little obvious economic capital are granted neither economic nor political citizenship. Lisa Duggan's (2002) conceptualisation of 'homonormativity' is important here and indicates the centrality of normalising discourses to sexual politics within neo-liberal governance. For Duggan, the increasing commercialisation and domesticity of gay culture has led to its depoliticisation through a focus on individual rights and freedoms, and practices of self-regulation and surveillance.

In *Profit and Pleasure: Sexual Identity in Late Capitalism*, Hennessy (2000) presents a trenchant critique of the global commodification of sexuality, which links gay marriage to market forces. The ever-extending 'gay marriage market' illustrates these points: hotels and wedding venues offer same-sex wedding packages; gift, flower, catering and card industries cater specially for same-sex couples; the travel industry offers gay-friendly honeymoons; and publishing companies ensure that magazines such as *DIVA* (aimed at lesbians) and *Gay Times* (aimed at gay men) capitalise on advertising revenue from the above industries. Gay marriage, then, is big business and, accordingly, formalising partnerships are an expensive endeavour. Yvette Taylor's (2007) empirical work on the intersections of social class and sexuality thus indicates that decisions around whether or not to civilly partner are often materially guided. Taylor wryly proposes that:

> The problem with civil partnerships it would seem, is much like the problem with a wedding itself. It's all well and good in theory, it's heavenly to look through the magazines and dream of the special day and all the joy it will bring, but what happens when the fireworks are over, how does one translate marital dreams into practical, civil reality? And what happens if you can't afford the white wedding in the first place? What if your gift list is a copy of the Argos catalogue?
>
> Taylor (2008: 2)

Taylor's research, moreover, shows that the benefits afforded by the CPA impacted very differently along class lines:

> For many working-class lesbians and gays, civil partnerships may mean little at best, given that extension of pension rights, one of the most tangible and practical benefits of the new arrangement, are less likely to apply. Conversely, it can be argued that the implications and consequences of civil partnerships may actually be restrictive and penalising for some working-class partnerships. One example of this, and for those in receipt of benefits quite a major change, is that when either partner in a same-sex couple applies for a means tested state benefit, the income of both partners will be taken into account.
>
> Taylor (2008: 2)

Especially in times of austerity the divide between cohabitation and marriage can be seen to be drawn along class lines rather than those of sexuality. Mandy Merk draws similar conclusions in her discussion of the recession hit United Kingdom: 'In these circumstances, postponing marriage and childbearing has increasingly become the norm in the United Kingdom, with the new homosexual familialism often remarked ironically as the sole countervailing trend' (2007: 62).

Along similar lines, research participant, Cheryl, spoke about her fears for diversity law in a culture of austerity:

> One of the things that people don't realise is that most of the civil rights that we have won have been won because society has become more affluent and if we were to get back to a stage where people are desperately looking to scrape a living then there will be much more... Looking for scapegoats...
>
> (Cheryl, age 51)

Cheryl's points here are significant; rights can be taken away as well as awarded. A further – and differently politically positioned – critique has been levelled at the CPA from other sections of lesbian and gay communities. From this perspective the CPA was seen to be lacking in its premise of equality. Thus the CPA was an inferior copy of partnership recognition and represented a dual system of rights. Peter Tatchell of *Outrage*, for example, likened the CPA to sexual apartheid: 'By legislating a two-tier system of relationship recognition Labour has, in effect, created a form of legal apartheid based on sexual orientation' (Tatchell, 2005). Likewise, Nancy Fraser (2003) argues that permitting civil unions for same-sex couples while denying them marriage perpetuates status inequality. Fraser subsequently argues that social justice may lie in one of two solutions: either the legalisation of same-sex marriage or the deinstitutionalisation of different-sex marriage (Thompson, 2006).

Fraser's latter proposed route to recognition parity – de-institutionalising heterosexual marriage – resonates with emerging legal and policy debates in the United Kingdom and is echoed in the demands of some social movements. In this way, Tatchell proposes a 'civil-commitment pact', which recognises, and affords rights to, a diversity of intimate relationships. This would, he argues 'allow people to nominate as their next of kin and beneficiary any "significant other" in their life. It could be a lover, but it could also be a sister, carer, housemate or lifelong best friend' (Tatchell, 2005). He continues:

> We see around us a huge variety of relationships and lifestyles. There are couples who live together, and those who live apart. Some share their finances; others maintain financial independence. The law should reflect and support these diverse

> relationship choices. The one-size-fits-all model of relationship recognition – exemplified by marriage and civil partnerships – is no longer appropriate.
>
> Tatchell (2005)

In 2006 the UK Law Commission conducted a review of the legal rights of cohabiting couples, estimated at two million (Merk, 2007). The review considered the formalisation of property inheritance on death, the division of assets on separation and financial support for children in both these circumstances. In the United States, concerns around health care for cohabiting couples fuel similar debates. Writing on the impact of HIV and AIDS in the States, Judith Butler (2004) argues for the separation of economic benefits and marital status. Such moves are strongly contested by most religious bodies and especially the Catholic Church, which argues that a framework of partnership recognition in addition to marriage for heterosexual couples will dilute the latter. Even more contentious is Fraser's second route to social justice – that of same-sex marriage. While the issue of heterosexual non-marital recognition is gaining some ground at political and social movement levels, as discussed above, it is overshadowed, in both degrees of controversy and levels of support, by proposals for same-sex marriage.

Since the induction of the CPA in 2004 in the United Kingdom, sexual social movements stepped up their demands for same-sex marriage. In December 2012, the UK Conservative-Lib Dem Coalition Government announced their decision to introduce legislation to lift the ban on same-sex marriage in England and Wales in both civil and religious ceremonies. Similar plans had already been proposed in Scotland. Despite deep dissent from some Conservative Ministers and constituency members, and from religious bodies, 'The Marriage (Same-Sex Couples) Bill' was introduced into UK Parliament and had its first reading on 24 January 2013. At the Bill's second reading on the 5 February 2013, the House of Commons voted in favour of new legislation. To appease religious organisations, the Bill has the caveat that religious bodies who do not want to conduct same-sex marriages may opt out without legal challenge. Prime Minister David Cameron reported that the vote was 'an important step forward that strengthens society' (2013), while Deputy Prime Minister and Lib Dem Leader Nick Clegg subsequently stated: 'I genuinely believe that we will look back on today as a landmark for equality in Britain. [...] No matter who you are and who you love, we are all equal. Marriage is about love and commitment, and it should no longer be denied to people just because they are gay' (2013). 'The Equality Network', the UK equality charity that organised the campaign for same-sex marriage, similarly recounted the importance of legal parity:

> This is an historic day and a huge step forward for equality. After centuries of facing prejudice and discrimination, lesbian, gay, bisexual and transgender people can finally look forward to a day when they are no longer treated as second-class citizens.
>
> French (2013)

A language of 'sameness' and a discourse of normalisation are, then, clearly evident in both the campaign for, and the defence and support of, equal marriage. In this way, there exists a common language between a dominant stand of lesbian and gay political movement and government and policy makers (see also Richardson and Monro, 2012). As Richardson and Monro evocatively suggest:

> Lesbians and gay men were previously constrained by representations of themselves as mad, bad or sad; it would seem that now they are being shaped through normative constructions of responsible and respectable sexual citizens.
>
> Richardson and Monro (2012: 83)

In the passage considered above from Tom French's speech, 'Equality Network' widens the language of equality to include bisexual and trans people. The support for equal marriage gained much support from transgender organisations as it was seen as a potential solution to the problematics of the divorce clause in the GRA, as discussed above. In an interview with online gay news network 'PinkNews' during his campaign for leadership of the UK Labour Party in 2010, Ed Milliband also drew connections between the inequalities of gay and lesbians not being able to marry and trans married couples having to divorce:

> 'Separate but equal' is not good enough and PinkNews.co.uk's own recent poll demonstrated the huge support in the LGBT

> community for a right to marry. The cruel consequence of the current compromise is trans people forced to divorce their partners before they could be legally recognised in their new gender. I want to see heterosexual and samesex partnerships put on an equal basis and a Labour Party that I lead will campaign to make gay marriage happen.
>
> Milliband cited in Follon and Sayers (2011)

Yet, as James Morton from the campaigning organisation, 'The Scottish Transgender Alliance', argues, trans people will only benefit from equal marriage if the GRA is revised:

> It simply isn't equal marriage unless there is an amendment to the Gender Recognition Act. If the issue of transsexual requirement to divorce is not dealt with, we have not implemented equal marriage.
>
> Morton, cited in Follon and Sayers (2011)

It is to be seen whether the GRA will be revised in light of moves towards marriage equality, and whether the marriages that were dissolved in the 'forced choice' required by the divorce clause in the GRA, will be reinstated. These issues are certain to be central to transgender recognition politics in future years. Yet, as the chapter now moves on to consider, while issues around partnership recognition and equal marriage continue to gain political momentum, a parallel politics is concurrently being played out at both theoretical and substantive levels.

I don't: Refusing marriage; resisting love; rejecting the child

Central to early feminist theory and politics was a critique of 'compulsory heterosexuality' (Rich, 1980) and, particularly, of marriage as a political, economic and cultural institution through which men dominate women (MacKinnon, 1982). Similarly, sexual politics were articulated against dominant gendered relations and practices of intimacy, especially marriage and traditional family arrangements. The nuclear family was seen to be a restrictive and closeting environment at best, and, at worst, a practice of institutionalised homophobia. Jay and Young reflect on these earlier critiques of the nuclear family:

> The nuclear family, with its man-woman model built in by the presence of parents, is the primary means by which this restricted sexuality is created and enforced. Gays experience rejection by the family in a society where familial love is considered important. The family oppresses women and children as well as gays. The phenomena of runaway teenagers and increasing divorce rates are signs of the erosion of the nuclear family. Gay liberation is another sign. We attack the nuclear family when we refuse to get married and have a family. We are committed to building communal situations where children can grow strong and free.
>
> Jay and Young (1992)

A marriage critique was, moreover, attuned to intersectional inequalities – to the ways in which dominant structures depended upon the inequalities of, for example, class and race, in order to maintain hegemony. As Christopher Carrington (2009) argued in respect of his study into lesbian and gay families: 'Many of the affluent lesbigay families create a greater sense of equality between the partners through reliance on the service economy, or in other words, upon the poorly paid labours of others, notably women of color and younger less – educated gay men and lesbians' (1999: 215). Along similar lines, Taylor's work on lesbian and gay parenting (2009) illustrates the ways in which class bestows differing degrees of social and cultural capital to influence parenting 'choices'. These are important cautionary notes to add to the body of work suggesting a more democratic ethic of care structures in same-sex partnerships (Weston, 1991; Dunne, 1999; Weeks et al., 2001).

Early feminism and sexual movements, then, politicised the domestic sphere; heterosexuality, marriage, the nuclear family, gendered and parental relations were foregrounded as political issues. By turn, living outside traditional structures was seen to be not only personally beneficial but also politically strategic. Thus, in her critique of 'compulsory heterosexuality', Rich (1980) offers lesbianism not only as a sexual choice for women but also as a political solution to patriarchy. Moreover, sexual dissidents carved out a range of 'life experiments' (Weeks, 2007) in sexual and intimate spheres. Feminist and sexual historians have subsequently commented on the ways in which 'the family' was restructured to create 'families of choice' (Weston, 1991), which provided networks of care beyond those limited by biology or family line (see Hines, 2007a). Davina Cooper's point that understandings of equality from a diversity perspective often ignore 'equality's relationship to other social norms' (2004: 92) rings true here, bringing to mind the previous challenges to marriage that are forgotten in present equality moves. Cooper (2004) considers the ways in which prevailing norms create subordinate conditions for those who fail or refuse to live their lives in agreement, saying of same-sex partnership recognition: 'Arguably, this is where spousal recognition will have its most intensely felt effects, as non-monogamous relationships, casual sexual partners, celibacy and serial coupledom become officially separated from those couples "doing the right thing"' (2004: 116). Importantly, Cooper stresses that living outside of normative structures is a material, as well as discursive, process that has consequences across a number of arenas 'immigration entitlements, insurance premiums, personal taxation, state welfare, inheritance, access to certain goods and services, and the right to make, and be subject to, others' decisions' (2004: 116).

These points bring to mind Gayle Rubin's (1989) writing on the ordering of the 'sexual hierarchy'. Thus hierarchies of sexual value bestow privilege on members of the 'charmed circle' and penalise those on the 'outer limits', working to 'rationalize the well-being of the sexually privileged and the adversity of the sexual rabble' (Rubin, 1989: 152). Moreover, the maintenance of each category relies on the other through 'the need to draw and maintain an imaginary line between good and bad sex' (Rubin, 1989: 152), with tensions surfacing about where to draw the line. While the constituents of each category, then, are open to contestation and subject to social and cultural change, the categories themselves remain to discursively and materially structure sexual and intimate lives. In Rubin's schema, homosexuality and transsexualism were placed in the outer limits. Twenty years later, this is less pronounced and more complexly ordered as certain practices of homosexuality and, arguably, transgender have moved into the charmed circle. Nevertheless – and because of – others are resolutely delineated to the 'outer limits'. These issues connect with debates around sexual citizenship that will be considered in Chapter 6.

Offsetting the focus on intimate equality through legislative change as discussed above, recent research indicates a counter-tendency among sections of gender and sexual movements. Gavin Brown's (2007) ethnographic study of autonomous queer spaces in London points to the ways in which the reordering of gender, sexual and intimate relationships are considered part of the anti-capitalist project – though see Wilkinson's (2009) questioning of the extent to which gendered and sexual hierarchies and values are genuinely transformed within such spaces. Similarly, empirical work on non-monogamy and polyamoury, and asexuality, indicates the transformation of normative gendered and sexual ordering in intimate sites (see the diverse chapters in the collection on non-monogamies edited by Barker and Langdridge (2010), Klesse's (2007) empirical work on polyamoury, and Carrigan's (2012) work on asexuality). This strain of scholarship and activism stands in sharp contrast to the equalities agenda previously discussed. Rather, it echoes a queer politics of non-conformity and anti-assimilationism.

The work of American writer Lee Edelman unequivocally stands in opposition to discourses of 'sameness' and normalisation. For Edelman a queer politics is dependent upon the rejection of reproductive futurism: '*queerness* names the side of those *not* "fighting for the children," the side outside the consensus by which all politics confirms the absolute value of reproductive futurism' (2004: 3). Read in the context of a dominant politics that centres on same-sex marriage, parenting and reproductive rights, Edelman's call to 'fuck "the child" ' may initially refresh. Edelman, though, goes further in arguing that the queer subject is inextricably defined by that which is negative and non-productive. Rather than responding with calls for equality and recognition, Edelman urges queers to embrace negativity and non-futurity. For Edelman, standing outside reproductive futurism entails standing outside of futurism itself: 'Fuck Laws both with capital ls and with small; fuck the whole network of symbolic relations and the future that serves as its prop' (2004: 29).

Here 'queerness' embraces the death drive: the place of 'no future', to arrive at Bersani's (1987) anti-social space. Edelman's nihilistic queer gaze may be countered by turning to queer theorists, such as Warner, for whom queer theory *is* political: 'social justice is at the heart of queer theory' (Warner, 1993: xxvi). Sedgwick (1993) too demands that sexuality scholars retain a political analysis in order to address the intersections of gender, race, class and nationality in the upholding of sexual inequalities. Increasing levels of visibility and, for some, inclusion of gender and sexual diversity in the global North has been met by a call for a renewed queer politics that attends to a changed world order. In asking 'What's Queer About Queer Studies Now?', Eng, Halberstam and Munoz articulate 'queer' not as a synonym for same-sex identification or practice, but as a political and theoretical tool, arguing for a 'renewed queer studies' (Eng et al., 2005: 84). This speaks to, and offsets, Cohen's (2000) critique of the depoliticising of queer in demanding that queer politics readdress oppressions of gender, race and social class. Paradoxically, then, the mainstreaming of 'diversity' has reopened space for a range of transformative gender and sexual movements and provided a renewed impetus for critical queer analysis, offering moments of productive negativity (Halberstam, 2008).

Resonating with a politics of non-assimilationism, an 'anti-marriage' standpoint is currently gaining force, as illustrated in the following quotation from sexual activist Nair:

> I don't get why a community of people who have historically been fucked over by their families and the state now consists of people who want those exact same institutions to validate their existence. I think marriage is the gay Prozac, the drug of choice for gaysbians today: It makes them forget that marriage isn't going to give everyone health care, it won't give us a subsistence wage, it won't end all these fucked up wars that are killing people everywhere else.
>
> Nair (2009)

From this perspective, state relationship recognition and the notion of marriage itself are rebuffed for their heteronormative underpinnings. Clear links are made with radical sexual politics of the past. These themes are apparent in the work of Nicola Barker, whose book *Not the Marrying Kind: A Feminist Critique of Same-Sex Marriage* (2012) applies earlier feminist critiques of heterosexual marriage, as discussed above, to argue against same-sex marriage. There is also a growing body of scholarship that stands against what Eleanor Wilkinson (2012) terms 'compulsory romantic love'. Building on the work of Adrienne Rich (1980) on 'compulsory heterosexuality' and of Chris Ingraham (1996) on the 'heterosexual imaginary', both concepts of which bring to light the ways in which heterosexuality is ideologically naturalised, Wilkinson argues that it is the 'romantic imaginary' that works to discriminate in contemporary society. Norms of romantic love, she argues, are as deep-set within queer communities as they are within heterosexual spaces. Drawing on empirical research, Wilkinson illustrates the pressures on single people at individual and societal levels. Subsequently, she argues that:

> The privileging of sexual romantic attachments raises some key issues when it comes to rights claims and citizenship status, particularly the ways in which the romantic couple takes priority over other forms of attachment such as friendship.
>
> Wilkinson (2012: 142)

In *Single: Arguments for the Uncoupled,* Michael Cobb (2012) also writes about couple-culture's anxiety over, and around, single people – a panic which subsides only through erasing single status: 'there are no *real* single people out there – they're all just waiting for the chance to find that special someone, sometime soon. Everyone is pre- or post-couple. No one is *really* supposed to be single' (2012: 5). Cobb's point speaks to the absence of claims and citizenship status for single people that Wilkinson cautions against: there can be no recognition if the subject goes unrecognised.

Alongside the participants' narratives addressed in Chapter 4, which refuted gender recognition – those that I suggested indicate a politics of 'non-recognition' – the political positions, theoretical analyses and intimate practices that have been considered in the latter sections of this chapter signpost a strong countertendency to a politics of recognition, indicating transformative ways of living and loving that ask salient questions about the value of state recognition.

Conclusion

This chapter has considered a range of theoretical approaches and political positionings in relation to the recognition of intimate relationships in current times. In examining the dual development of the UK 2004 GRA and 2004 CPA the chapter drew out excluding mechanisms in current legal frameworks for trans people – notably those who wish to remain married to their pre-transition partners.

My empirical research shows that the divorce criteria in the GRA came under much criticism from research participants and is currently a key area of concern for transgender campaigning organisations. While a group of participants had benefitted from the Act as they were now able to marry in their acquired gender, participants who remained married to their pre-transition partners spoke angrily about having to choose between marriage to their long-standing partners and gender recognition. While it was felt that civil partnerships worked for transgender people who were in same-sex relationships, I suggested that linking the CPA and the GRA as the government has done in defence of the divorce clause shows a lack of understanding of the complex relationship between gender and sexuality, and enacts new practices of inequality – thus hampering moves to recognise intimate diversity.

Latter sections of the chapter explored two very different routes to social justice. The first seeks to expand frameworks of recognition in order to bring about increased levels of legal equality. Campaigns for equal marriage, I suggested, sit squarely within this route. The second rejects formalisation and critiques processes of normalisation. Here, I drew on an array of analytical, political and substantive moments of refusal – conceptualising these as instances of a politics of 'non-recognition'. The momentum of refusal from these movements is fuelled by an analysis of power relations – a political awareness that getting married, or becoming recognised as a man or woman, will do little to alleviate systems of power that structure inequalities of gender, race and class. Moreover, such critiques point to the ways in which new exclusions are enacted as the disenfranchised become further marginalised in the latest hierarchies of 'belonging'. To 'choose' not to belong is thus to align with those who 'can't belong'. These themes underscore debates about citizenship and equality governance, which will be drawn out in Chapter 6.

6
Governing Diversity

Introduction

This chapter contextualises previous discussions of the UK GRA within UK equality and diversity law and policy more broadly. Over the last decade in the United Kingdom five pieces of legislation have been passed in relation to gender and sexuality: the Sexual Offences (Amendment) Act (2000); the Adoption and Children Act (2002); the GRA (2004); the CPA (2004) and the Equality Act (2006, 2010). As illustrated in Chapter 3 in respect of the GRA, new legislation based on issues of gender and sexuality equality follows on from the HRA (1998). Conversely, the passing of the HRA cannot be separated from a post-1997 culture in which notions of 'equality', 'diversity' and 'citizenship' became articulated anew – concepts which are central to recognition politics.

This chapter begins by addressing the UK New Labour Government's utilisation of the concepts of equality and diversity. Here I explore the ways in which discourses of sameness and difference are problematically employed in recent legal and policy frameworks. These issues are further drawn out as the chapter turns to debates around citizenship. The next section of the chapter links back to discussions in previous chapters about assimilation as it explores discourses of 'sameness' in equality and diversity law and policy.

The chapter then moves on to consider recent empirical studies, which have examined the institutional implementation of equality and diversity discourse and policy (Ahmed, 2012; Richardson and Monro, 2012). The last section of the chapter employs empirical material from my own research to consider the winners and losers in gender and sexual recognition politics. The chapter assesses how new laws speak to critical citizenship studies and gauges the relevance of these arguments in light of recent law and policy. Here critiques are brought to bear on the law for reproducing dichotomous frameworks, which reproduce hierarchies of hetero/homo and binaries of male/female. The chapter thus examines how new forms of gendered and sexuality inequality are patterned; the political implications of which will be explored in Chapter 7.

Legislating for equality and diversity

At the start of 2007, the UK 'Commission for Equality and Human Rights' elected the year as the 'year of equal opportunities', as the statement from their website shows:

> The Commission has designated 2007 as 'European Year of Equal Opportunities for All' as part of a concerted effort to promote equality and non-discrimination in the EU. It is designed to give a focus to tackling discrimination, celebrating diversity and promoting equal opportunities for all.
>
> (equalityhumanrights.com)

At this time the United Kingdom certainly saw a flurry of activity around gender and sexual equality within social policy and the law. By 2007, the new millennium had witnessed the passing of five pieces of legislation that explicitly addressed gender and sexuality within the context of human rights and equality: first, the Sexual Offences (Amendment) Act (2000), which equalised the age of consent for lesbians, gay men, bisexuals and heterosexuals to 16 in England, Wales and Scotland, and 17 in Northern Ireland; second, the Adoption and Children Act (2002), which enabled same-sex and unmarried couples to apply for joint adoption in England and Wales; third, as discussed throughout previous chapters, the GRA (2004), which granted transsexual people the right to change their birth certificate and to marry in their acquired gender; fourth, as Chapter 5 explored, the CPA (2004), which granted lesbians, gay men and bisexuals the rights of civil marriage – including rights around property, inheritance tax, social security and pension benefits, the ability to get parental responsibility for a partner's children, tenancy rights, full life insurance recognition and next-of-kin rights in hospital – and finally, the Equality Act (2006, 2010), which brought together the three separate equality commissions – the Equal Opportunities Commission; the Commission for Racial Equality and the Disability Rights Commission – and addressed new legislation around discrimination on the basis of religion and faith, age and, significantly for the purposes of this book, sexual orientation. Discrimination on the grounds of sexual orientation, then, has only recently been legislated against and its inclusion makes illegal the discrimination of lesbians and gay men in the workplace. As discussed in Chapter 5, it is also likely that The Marriage (Same-Sex Couples) Bill (2013) will become law in the near future.

Irene Gedalof's (2013) policy analysis of UK equality documents examines New Labour's White Paper *Fairness For All,* which acted as the antecedent of the 2006, and then 2010, Equality Act. Gedalof outlines how the White Paper linked the organisational and legislative proposals in terms of the 'new challenges' facing contemporary UK society. Inequalities of gender, race, disability and sexuality were positioned as constraining both individual freedom and societal political and economic growth. In terms of the latter, the White Paper:

> strongly espoused the 'business case for diversity' arguing that discrimination against social groups runs counter to the needs of a modern globalised economy, and that a deep-rooted culture change that embraces diversity was needed. Similarly, the more recent moves towards a single Equality Act reiterated these assumptions about the ways which equality and diversity are central to both social cohesion and economic progress.
>
> Gedalof (2013: 3)

Taken together, discourse around equality and the recent legislative shifts emerging from recognition struggles could be read as representing a pathway to diversity and equality, symbolising a liberal and egalitarian 21st Century Britain, which has taken to heart – and to the Chamber – the political demands and the theoretical arguments of gender and sexual minorities. Such a position is largely reflected by Jeffrey Weeks (2007), who, in his recent book *The World We Have Won,* talks of a world of transformation – of a revolution that has transformed the possibilities of living gendered, intimate and erotic lives. Yet, as indicated in previous chapters and as this chapter moves on to explore in more detail, the recent legislative package around equality and diversity also suggests the need to be hesitant about a linear reading, which positions these moves as evidence that gender and sexual minorities as a whole are experiencing greater levels of recognition. These issues can be further explored through critical citizenship scholarship.

Critiquing gendered and sexual citizenship

Citizenship has been broadly defined as the collection of rights and responsibilities that establish political membership and enable access to benefits and resources (Hines, 2007a). Western notions of citizenship have traditionally followed a liberal model in which individual rights are stressed alongside minimum state intervention and market freedom (Marshall, 1950), yet, both understandings and practices of citizenship are deeply contested. While neo-conservatives argue that the balance between rights and duties is weighted too heavily in favour of the former, radical critics have variously pointed to how the rights of dominant social groups are protected at the expense of marginal groups (Hines, 2007a).

The latter perspectives propose a broader conceptualisation of citizenship in order to take greater account of marginalised groups. Work on citizenship, race and ethnicity – and the intersections with gender – (Back and Solomos, 2000; Lewis, 2000), for example, has illustrated how traditional models of citizenship have failed to take account of these social positionings. Thus dominant notions of citizenship presume a white subject, while citizenship discourse around immigration and multiculturalism stresses a language of sameness (to white UK citizens), as discussed above. Feminist critical citizenship scholarship has focused on how women's interests are neglected through a traditional model of citizenship that focused upon the 'private' (paid labour) rather than the 'personal' (domestic), thus marginalising women's interests in the latter – for example, in unpaid caring work (Lister, 1997). More broadly, feminist scholars (Pateman, 1989; Walby, 1994; Lister, 1997; Bussemaker and Voet, 1998; Daly and Cowen; 2000) have challenged assumptions of the citizen as male, pointing to the ways in which this presumption in dominant models of citizenship discriminates against the social positioning of women.

Work on citizenship from critical race and feminist scholars importantly links citizenship discourse to citizenship practice, showing how language actively constructs experience and meaning. To this effect, sexuality scholars have articulated the ways in which discourses of citizenship are constructed along a heterosexual model so that the notion of citizenship itself (and the citizen her/himself) is heterosexualised. Thus writers in sexuality studies (Evans, 1993; Cooper, 1995; Plummer, 1995; Richardson, 1998; Seidman, 1998; Bell and Binnie, 2000; Weeks, 2000; Weeks et al., 2004) have addressed how traditional models of citizenship mask difference; in this instance to marginalise the experiences and discriminate against the rights of those who variously live outside the hetero norm. Writers such as Carl Stychin (1998), Diane Richardson (1998), David Bell and Jon Binnie (2000) and Shane Phelan (2010), in particular, have focused upon the effects of citizenship discourses of sexual 'sameness'. Richardson argues that the granting of lesbian and gay rights leads to the privatisation and circumscription of these sexual identities: 'Lesbians and gay men are granted the right to be tolerated as long as they stay within the boundaries of that tolerance' (1998: 90).

Since notions of citizenship are heterosexualised, such boundaries of tolerance depend upon rights-based claims (such as the right to marry), which fit with a heterosexual model of the 'good citizen', as discussed in Chapter 5. Accordingly, Stychin points to the perils of articulating lesbian and gay rights through the concept of citizenship: 'lesbians and gays seeking rights may embrace an ideal of "respectability", a construction that then perpetuates a division between "good gays" and (disreputable) "bad queers".' (1998: 200). It is the latter who are excluded from notions of citizenship. Similarly, Bell and Binnie (2000) suggest that sexual citizenship implies a set of 'rights-based' claims, for example, the right for lesbians and gay men to marry and to serve in the military, which, in turn, entails a set of duties; notably the duty to assimilate. This constructs a binary between the 'good homosexual' (the assimilator) and the 'bad homosexual' (the dissident), with the former granted citizenship: 'The effect of this manoeuvre on activist strategies can be to surrender some "rights" for the sake of others' (Bell and Binnie, 2000: 204). More recently, work on transgender citizenship has explored how a universal gendered model of citizenship fails to account for gender diverse people (Monro, 2005; Hines, 2006a, 2007a; Hines and Sanger, 2010). Key here is how equality and diversity law and policy are developed on the premise of 'sameness'. By turn, recognition is granted on this basis and rights awarded to those who assimilate. With regard to transgender citizenship, this argument has been evidenced through the empirical material considered in previous chapters, which points to the ways in which only certain trans people's rights and means of recognition are enabled by the UK GRA As Richardson and Monro (2012) argue, despite recent legal shifts: 'citizenship is still largely constituted in terms of particular forms of (hetero)sexual relations as the yardstick for recognition' (Richardson and Monro, 2012: 65). We can add to this that citizenship remains constituted in terms of particular forms of gendered relations in order to account for continued gaps in transgender citizenship, as Emily Grabham (2007) argues in her work on the construction of intersex citizenship through particular forms of gendered embodiment. When issues of intersectional (in)equality are taken into account, particularly at the global level, a Western notion of sexual or intimate citizenship may be seen to be limited (see Binnie, 2004; Kulpa and Mizielińska, 2012). As Ken Plummer argues:

> Once low income societies and the poor of rich societies are brought into the picture the concept of intimate citizenship starts to demand further clarification. Looking at issues of abject poverty, forced marriages, sexual slavery, the commodification of bodies etc., intimate citizenship takes on wider meanings. For here are people who have little control over their bodies, feelings, relationships; little access to representations, relationships, public spaces etc; and few socially grounded choices about identities, gender experiences, erotic experiences.
>
> Plummer (1995: 25)

As Richardson and Monro (2012) propose, these points of critique show the importance of conceptualising citizenship beyond a politics of 'choice' and of being mindful of the power dynamics underpinning the state's granting of citizenship and recognition. Such a departure also requires a move away from universalist understandings of citizenship and rights, as explored in Chapter 3. Yet, as the next section of this chapter shows, this is not just a matter of reconceptualisation on academic and political-activist levels, since universalism is constructed through legal and policy discourses – and thus practices – of sameness.

Discourses of sameness and difference

In Chapters 4 and 5, I analysed the language of the UK GRA to argue that subjective understandings and everyday practices of gendered and sexual diversity, as illustrated by research participants, were hampered by a restrictive conceptualisation of diversity in the writing of the GRA. In Chapter 4, I argued that although the GRA represented a move beyond understanding gender as distinct from 'sex', its gender binary framework (and its demand that gender change should be lifelong) failed to take account of gender *diversity* – thus gendered practices outside of, or fluctuating between, the positions of male and female are not addressed in the law. Moreover, I argued that the evidence-based criteria of the Act instrumentally countered gender difference through demanding that a person be diagnosed with gender dysphoria before being deemed eligible for a Gender Recognition Certificate (GRC). This leaves transsexualism (rather than gender diversity per se) as the only permissible route to gender recognition and, as such, reproduces much critiqued medical understandings of transsexualism as pathological. Indeed, the GRA is the only law that demands that people certify as mentally ill before rights are awarded. This criterion leads many gender diverse people to reproduce a transsexual narrative strategically, for rights and benefits. Elsewhere (Hines, 2007a) I have discussed the 'wrong body' story as a 'rehearsed narrative' that is pragmatically applied. While people may access rights and benefits through this strategy, they are forced to identify with categories that are not their own and, as such, are misrecognised in law. In Chapter 5, I argued that the 'divorce' clause in the GRA legislated against intimate diversity in requiring that people in pre-transition marriages divorce. The tempering of diversity, I have argued, results from strategies of 'sameness', rather than a framework of difference. Gedalof argues likewise in her analysis of equality and diversity policy documents:

> The liberal notion of equality that underpins contemporary policy is premised on valuing sameness over difference. It does this in its taking of the autonomous, undifferentiated and

> universal individual and the basic unit of analysis, stripping away particularistic ties of kinship, sub-national community or 'culture', personal belief and tradition to reveal an essential sameness that we can all share as moral, economic or political actors. Particularistic ties of difference are safely housed in the space of the private, so that public issues of justice, rights and access to resources can be negotiated between undifferentiated individuals.
>
> Gedalof (2013: 4)

However, access to resources is differentiated and, so, as Gedalof (2013) subsequently points out, a language of equality is individualised depoliticised speech, which detracts from collective disadvantage and power inequalities. Moreover, as I have argued elsewhere (Hines, 2010), an examination of the discourse of law and policy is important since this language works to actively construct notions and requirements of citizenship, thus producing citizens themselves. In this instance, my work has examined how particular (trans) gendered citizens are produced through legal discourse (of the GRA), though there are many other parallel examples: the ways in which policy on multiculturalism and immigration works to ascertain sameness, through, for example, language/citizenship 'tests' or – to use the UK Government's jargon – the 'Life in the UK test' (2013). Thus, as Gedalof argues: 'Difference can only be accommodated if, first, there is a secure and stable ground of sameness upon which our differences can be allowed to flower' (2013: 7). *Diversity* itself, then, becomes diluted through equality and diversity discourse and, as I now move on to explore, through its implementation and institutionalisation.

Doing – and undoing – equality and diversity

The social movements of feminism and sexuality have, over the last five decades, impacted significantly on law and policy, particularly around work cultures and practices. The 'successes', then, of these social movements are frequently measured in terms of legal change. Thus the following are cited as evidence of the impacts of feminism: the Equal Pay Act, 1970; The Sex Discrimination Act, 1975; The Employment Protection Act, 1975; The Equal Pay (Amendment) Act, 1985; The Prohibition of Female Circumcision Act, 1985; The

Sex Discrimination (Amendment) Act, 1986; Independent Taxation, 1990; Criminalisation of Rape in Marriage, 1994; Parental Leave Legislation, 1999; The Female Genital Mutilation Act, 2003. Although legislative change around sexual equality was slower to be introduced, the post-1997 laws discussed above are often cited as evidence that sexual movements have 'made a difference'. While social movements have undoubtedly effected change, this sentiment assumes a progressive shift in cultural understandings and practices as a result of legal and policy change. This 'cause and effect' model is, though, very much open to question – for example, gay men and lesbians still get 'queer bashed' whether or not they are civilly partnered, and it is doubtful that those committing transphobic acts have heard of the GRA. Correspondingly, several participants talked about the ways in which the GRA was largely unknown, even within equalities and diversity fields. One research participant, Jennifer, who worked in social services reflected this:

> I don't think it is widely known that the Gender Recognition Act is out there. It's only sort of known even by those people who have got a handle on diversity. X [her local authority workplace] launched a diversity training course. And it did say in there about the Gender Recognition Act but I wouldn't have been surprised if people understood, they probably didn't understand what the title was never mind anything else. Because people don't think about gender identity. People are aware of gender, but... I organised as part of the LGBT network a speaker to come to our last meeting who spoke about there being seven diversity strands, you know, one being gender but another being gender identity and that there were some overlap but the two were distinct. And I don't think many people get that, that you can have a gender and that you can have a gender identity. People who are transgendered think about it every day, when you wake up... But people who don't have that mindset probably don't think about it.
>
> (Jennifer, age 36)

Here Jennifer refers to the 2010 Equality Act, which added 'gender reassignment' to sit alongside 'sex' as an equality strand; strands that are referred to as 'protected characteristics', which act as legislative shields against harassment, victimisation or discrimination. Further, the Act seeks to go beyond protection and enact change through public sector Equality Duty, which states that public bodies must have due regard to the need to: eliminate unlawful discrimination, harassment and victimisation; advance equality of opportunity; foster good relations between different groups. Yet, few participants felt that the GRA had any impact on their work lives. The vast majority felt that both the private and public sectors were unaware of the changing law. This view applied equally to work colleagues, human resources and organisational structures. Josie's view was commonplace: 'I really don't think anyone in my workplace has heard of the GRA. No one has ever mentioned it. No, nothing' (Josie, age 48). Although some participants talked about hoping that the GRA would be beneficial in relation to future discrimination in the workplace, others were more sceptical; thus Jo said: 'You get to work, you get sacked from your job, but no-one puts the trans word in the equation. Can you prove it was because you're trans? Well no, the GRA isn't going to help you' (Jo, age 45).

As Sara Ahmed says: 'in legislating for equality (and against inequality), it can be assumed that equality is achieved *in the act* [...] it is as if having a policy becomes a substitute for action' (2012: 10–11). Moreover, this presumes that law and policy moves are able to enact social and cultural changes'. Rather, as Jennifer indicated, awareness of equality and diversity policy is limited. Thus Ahmed importantly suggests that 'We might want to be cautious about the appealing nature of diversity and ask whether the ease of its incorporation by institutions is a sign of the loss of its critical edge' (2012: 1). Here it is helpful to turn to three recent studies on the institutionalisation and operation of equality and diversity.

In her study of the passage of narratives of discrimination to frameworks of entitlement, Davina Cooper (2004) writes of 'diversity':

> This space does not equate to an ideological or political stance. Rather, it is a broad, discursive space that emerged out of the very particular social, cultural and political conditions of the 1980s and 1990s – namely, the dismantling of the Soviet Union and of the communist regimes of eastern Europe, the upsurge of neo-liberal ideology.
>
> Cooper (2004: 5)

What is striking here is that the exact conditions are read as giving rise to a politics of diversity as those credited with leading to a politics of recognition by the recognition theorists discussed in Chapter 1. Cooper continues to name the following as further conditions of diversity politics:

> the backlash against radical feminism, the expansion of lesbian and gay politics, including the birth of Queer, and the struggles around multiculturalism and anti-racism.
>
> Cooper (2004: 5)

Here Cooper's discussion of diversity politics includes both the right-based claims of social movements, which, as previous chapters have explored, have also been firmly linked to recognition politics as well as those moments (the growth of a feminist critique of radical feminist approaches to transgender, and the development of Queer politics) that I have previously explored as sites of activism that stand apart from recognition politics. Cooper's analysis of diversity is interesting here, then, as it encompasses recognition and, what I have termed, moments of non-recognition. Moreover, for Cooper, a politics of diversity moves beyond discourses of 'tolerance' that resonate in equality speech. Rather, 'The space of diversity politics is one in which social diversity is valued and celebrated, not just within the private sphere but within public life and fora as well' (Cooper, 2004: 7). At this point, Cooper's sentiments read as counter to the points I have raised throughout this book concerning the assimilationist qualities of 'diversity', or in other words, the lack of diversity in diversity agendas. However, and this is my point in considering Cooper's points in detail, a different understanding emerges when the passage is contextualised in the time of its writing. As Cooper goes on to discuss, her use of 'diversity' intersects with that of 'difference' in order to 'highlight the relationship, but also the overlap between difference as a term of critique and diversity as a normative politics' (2004: 8). Reading this a decade on illustrates the extent of changes at conceptual, political, legal and policy levels, most notably, the linking of equality and diversity in government legal and policy forums. Thus my use of Cooper's work here is not with the intention of critique, but rather to illustrate the speed of which, and the extent to which, discursive spaces have shifted. As I address in Chapter 7, a politics of difference now reads very differently from the language of diversity.

Writing about her empirical research into the institutionalisation of diversity policy in higher education, Ahmed (2012) discusses the ways in which diversity practitioners distinguish between the language of diversity and that of equality. As Ahmed details, the institutional language of 'diversity' replaced earlier terms such as 'equal opportunities'. For many members of the equality sector, the term reflects a US managerialist organisational model of higher education, which is critiqued for corporatising the university. Ahmed, accordingly, states: 'The shift to the language of diversity could thus be understood in market terms; diversity has a commercial value and can be used as a way not only of marketing the university but of making the university into a marketplace' (2012: 52–53). Ahmed moves on to consider the utilisation of diversity as a management term: 'something to be managed and valued as a human resource' (2012: 53). At this level, diversity stands for individual differences, which can be systematically contained. In the context of Ahmed's research into racism and diversity, diversity thus becomes a way of managing the 'troubles' of multiculturalism. As Ahmed says, institutionalising diversity does not commit an institution to redressing systematic inequalities. Indeed, it may reflect a counter-tendency: 'the lack of commitment to change and might even allow organisations such as universities to conceal the operation of systematic inequalities.' (2012: 53). Diversity may thus become a smokescreen to mask difference. Ahmed develops this argument in considering diversity work through the concept of performativity: 'What is created by the description of the university as diverse might be the very idea of a university being diverse, which as an idea then circulates within the community that is being described. The "diverse university" becomes a shared object, if others within the university repeat the description; the repetition of the utterance gives it force' (Ahmed, 2012: 56). Yet, the upshot of the performativity of diversity is often that which is 'non-performative' – diversity discourse fails to act what it speaks.

I suggest that the performativity – and non-performative – qualities of diversity discourse is especially evident in the post-1997 turn to equality and diversity. In relation to diversity work in higher education, Ahmed, illustrates how the development of diversity documents often becomes a substitute for diversity action. Again, this is synonymous with neo-liberal governance; here the 'documents' are equality laws and policy, which fail to ascribe the gendered and sexual diversity that is discursively evoked. As Ahmed points out, because the term diversity is 'everywhere' does not mean that it is realised. This is particularly the case when diversity is operationalised through performance indicators. Here, diversity becomes an institutional target, which is, accordingly, subject measurement. As Ahmed says, the principle of having an institution accounting for its equitable standards is, in itself, no bad thing. The problem is, though, that diversity becomes yet another target among many and diversity becomes a self-serving tick-box exercise rather than a means through which to bring about greater levels of equality: 'when equality becomes another performance indicator, it cannot be treated outside the disciplinary regimes, whose ends might not be consistent with equality understood as a social aim or aspiration' (Ahmed, 2012: 85).

Diane Richardson and Surya Monro's (2012) empirical work on the implementation of sexuality equality and diversity policy in local government also found that measuring diversity is central to the rolling out of equality initiatives in decentralised local government. Their study concurs with Ahmed's in that the measuring of equality and diversity often works to obstruct, rather than motivate, implementation of the wider goals of such policy. Equality and diversity performance indicators were thus identified by Richardson and Monro as a barrier and form of resistance to change (2012: 127). Though their research found evidence of positive aspects of organisational change in relation to equality and diversity policy – most notably, when underpinned by practitioner training and strong leadership – barriers to change occurred across different levels: 'compliance' – doing what has to be done without pro-activity; 'omission' – feeling unable to make change; 'erasure' – questioning the need; and active resistance – opposition to equality and diversity policy. Richardson and Monro identified 'compliance' in relation to LGBT issues as a gap between policy and practice. Resonating with Ahmed's (2012) findings discussed above, Richardson and Monro found that while these issues were emphasised in policy documentation, they were not translated into practice. 'Omission' occurred when practitioners experienced institutional barriers, to acting on policy recommendations. Such barriers often relate to limited resources, though other aspects were identified by Richardson and Monro as particularly evident in relation to sexualities and transgender equalities policy, including 'affective and moral issues, which could result in ambivalence towards taking the LGBT equalities agenda forward. In particular – being "personal" and belonging in the "private sphere" appeared to be particularly salient barriers to sexualities and trans equalities work' (Richardson and Monro, 2012: 130). As Richardson and Monro say, these points link with Shona Hunter's (2011) work on the affective dynamics of equality and diversity policy – that which Hunter terms 'impossible governance'. Davina Cooper's (2004) work on equality is also relevant here in showing the ways in which equalities agenda's may be blocked by unsympathetic managers.

Richardson and Monro's third category of resistance is that of 'erasure'. Here they refer to issues of distancing and (in)visibility – for example, one of their interviewees spoke about sitting in a meeting with councillors who stated that there were no LGBT employees in the Council and so sexualities and transgender equalities policy was deemed insignificant (Richardson and Monro, 2012: 132). Finally, Richardson and Monro's scale of resistance accounts for 'active opposition':

> Despite the legislative and policy shifts that have occurred over the last decade there was evidence of resistance to change that went beyond ambivalence about LGBT equalities associated with lack of knowledge or feelings of discomfort, where people were still acting on very basic and clearly unsubstantiated prejudice and being deliberatively obstructive.
>
> Richardson and Monro (2012: 135)

Central to the Equality Act (2006) was the positioning of equalities legislation as a 'public' duty. As Sara Ahmed's and Diane Richardson and Surya Monro's research shows, however, inscribing a 'public' duty does not erase 'private' prejudice (Richardson and Monro, 2012). Linking with the issues discussed earlier in this chapter, Richardson and Monro's research also brings to light the tensions between the recognition of difference and an equalities agenda that emphasises values of universality and sameness: 'there is an apparent tension in the extent to which differences and the complex social locations within group membership may be acknowledged. This may mean that intersecting inequalities such as those of gender, race, class and disability, for instance, are not addressed' (2012:34). Thus, as I have argued at several points in this book, discourses of 'sameness' work to block diversity. Richardson and Monro's work intersectionally stresses the ways in which structural changes regarding sexual and gender minority are complexly and differentially experienced along lines of class, gender, sexuality, age, race and ethnicity, and nationality, among other identities (2012: 176). Moreover, discussions in this and previous chapters indicate the ways in which some members of gendered and sexual minority groups are able to *be* more equal than others. A connected issue is the erasure of difference within, and among, marginalised communities through equalities and diversity law and policy. Brian Heaphy's (2008) work is significant here in showing how the acronym LGBT works to remove the specificities of difference in and between the 'L', the 'G', the 'B' and the 'T'. This is notably the case with the inclusion of 'T' within this acronym. While the 'adding on' of 'T' works in relation to lesbian, gay or bisexual trans people, it is often read as problematic by heterosexual trans people. In this way, the additive may be read as the continued misreading of transgender as an issue of sexuality, rather than of gender. This is particularly problematic given the long-standing pathologisation of transgender as a sexual 'disorder' (see Hines, 2007b).

A further difficulty with the institutionalisation of equality and diversity agendas lies with what Pete Dwyer (2004) has termed 'conditionality'. Dwyer' s argument focuses broadly on New Labour's welfare reforms, though is highly applicable to the underpinnings of new frameworks for citizenship in the United Kingdom that have been the subject of this chapter. Characteristic of recent reforms is a conditional entitlement to benefits and resources, or, to use Dwyer's turn of phrase, 'no rights without responsibilities' (Dwyer, 2004: 265). Janice McLaughlin et al. illustrate how this may work with regards to LGBT citizenship and politics of recognition:

> The mechanisms and institutional responses to recognition appear to be producing new or altered forms of 'conditionality' within

> rights and citizenship. By that we mean that groups and individuals need to 'prove' that they should be recognised by the state in certain ways in order to claim resources and legitimacy.
>
> McLaughlin et al. (2011: 1)

Reported instances – and the fears that such stories generate at community levels – of GRCs being demanded as 'proof' of gender, in relation to the use of toilet facilities, for instance, take the points of McLaughlin et al. one step further. Thus 'proving' operates as a multifaceted process – from the individual to the state and back to the wider community. One participant, Cheryl referred to this incidence:

> The point of the GRA was to allow trans people to operate as normal people in society, not to give them some sort of special identity card which they have to keep showing in order to get decent treatment from the authorities.
>
> (Cheryl, age 51)

This also indicates the very problematic ways in which recognition may be used to mark boundaries and police gendered practices within communities. These battles are often fought around questions of authenticity and indicate the ways in which dominant members of marginalised communities may seek to regulate the less powerful. These points link back to debates around identity politics from Chapter 4.

As McLaughlin et al. argue, central to recognition pathways are processes of normalisation, which depend upon reducing difference through a demand for 'sameness'. As previous chapters of this book have suggested, such a strategy is strongly apparent in the criterion set out in the GRA. Thus successful applicants are ones who fit with normative understandings of gender identity and of female and male embodiment. Moreover, as I have argued in this chapter, successful applicants are ones who fit standard configurations of intimacy. As I have suggested elsewhere (Hines, 2009), law and policy does not simply represent sexual and gendered subjects, it brings them into being; reconstructing gender and sexual identities and subjectivities anew. Richardson and Monro argue similarly in their discussion of 'the normal' lesbian/gay citizen who is 'in the process of being materialized primarily through an adherence to dominant intimate norms coded as heterosexual and monogamous. It is "the couple" within a particular domesticated setting that has become the rights bearing subject of lesbian and gay claims to citizenship' (Richardson and Monro, 2012: 81). Normalising processes do not only bring particular subjects into view – and, by turn, leave others in the shadows – they also work at the levels of the subjective and imaginary, bringing into focus – or, diminishing – what and who is possible.

Conclusion

This chapter has considered the UK GRA alongside broader UK gender and sexual equalities and diversity law and policy that has been developed over the last decade. The early section of this chapter discussed how a distinct framework of equalities law and policy was initiated under the UK New Labour Government. Concepts of 'equality', 'diversity' and 'citizenship' became newly articulated in relation to gender and sexuality – concepts which were addressed as being central to recognition politics.

In addressing the UK New Labour Government's utilisation of equality and diversity, the chapter explored the ways in which notions of 'sameness' work to guide normalising discourse and practices. These issues were further apparent as the chapter addressed debates around citizenship and assimilation. Recent conceptual and empirical studies examining the ways in which UK equality and diversity policy has been institutionalised and implemented were applied alongside my own research findings to evaluate diversity's success. Here I argued that 'diversity' is frequently diluted in the 'doing' of equalities and diversity work. Recent legal and policy shifts around gender and sexuality were seen to produce dichotomous frameworks, which reinstate old – and bring into being, new – hierarchies. New forms of gendered and sexuality inequality can thus be seen to be patterned through an equality and diversity drive.

This chapter indicates that the implementation of UK equality law and policy is a haphazard and uneven terrain. In particular, there are deep fissures between the development of law and policy and its operation 'on the ground'. Thus a neo-liberal human discourse of citizenship and recognition privileges the rights of individuals and social groups who are able and/or willing to conform to normative modes of being. Moreover, these arguments shed light on how liberal universalism glosses over the ways in which the desire for citizenship and recognition is complexly situated. I suggest, then, that if 'diversity' is to be taken seriously, neither a politics nor a theoretical framework of gendered and sexual citizenship and/or recognition is adequate to account for – and service – gender and sexual diversity. It is from this juncture that Chapter 7 instates a politics of difference.

7
From Recognition to a Politics of Difference

Introduction

In Chapter 1, I explored the UK GRA in relation to the role of 'recognition' within recent social movements and political theory. This book began, then, by contextualising recognition alongside the fracturing of social democratic ideals and the rise of identity politics and new social movements from the late 1960s. Chapter 1 looked in detail at key theorists in the recognition literature, setting out their distinct approaches to recognition and, by turn, to social justice. These debates were evaluated through empirical data from my research exploring the impact and significance of the GRA.

Understandings, politics and practices of recognition ran through subsequent chapters of the book, which considered theories of recognition in relation to human rights, social movement theory and identity politics, sociologies of intimacy and queer theory, citizenship, and equality and diversity discourse. Throughout Chapters 2–6, I have thus assessed the relevance of recognition theory and politics for gender and sexual diversity, particularly in relation to transgender identities, subjectivities and embodiment. While themes central to understandings and practices of recognition have been apparent to these questions and have, to different degrees, resonated with the empirical material I employed to further analyse recognition debates, on many occasions I have found both a theory and a politics of recognition to be unsatisfactory for accounting for gender diversity. In this respect, this chapter begins by summarising the main points of my argument.

The chapter moves on to examine Iris Marion Young's (1990, 2000) work on a politics of difference. This framework, I suggest, holds much greater potential for enabling social justice in relation to gender and sexuality than does the notion of recognition. The second section of this chapter sets out my argument here and examines how a politics of difference may work to redress the problematics apparent in the language and practices of recognition, human rights and citizenship, as discussed in previous chapters.

The limits of recognition

Intersectionalities

In considering the recognition literature in Chapter 1, I addressed the debate, particularly between Nancy Fraser and Judith Butler, concerning distinctions between politics of redistribution and ones of recognition. To recap, for Fraser, though each is important in bringing about social justice, the constituents of each are particular: a politics of redistribution seeks to reorder the share of material resources, while a politics of representation aims to shift cultural understandings and representations. Fraser (1997) positions politics of social class in the former and politics of sexuality in the latter. Judith Butler (1998) challenged what she read as Fraser's understanding of sexuality as 'merely cultural'; pointing to the ways in which sexuality intersects with material concerns. I also considered Iris Marion Young's (1997) critique of Fraser at length here. In evaluating these debates, I argued that the economic/cultural dichotomy that ran through recognition theory led to it being limited as a political model through which to agitate for transgender rights. Rather, I argued for an intersectional account of the economic and the cultural (see also Hines, 2010) for an analysis of the intersections of gender and sexuality in relation to transgender).

Alongside my previous research on transgender practices of identity, intimacy and care (Hines, 2007a), the research project 'Gender Diversity, Recognition and Citizenship' on the impact and significance of the UK GRA, which informs this book, indicates the multifarious ways in which material and cultural forces shape transgender subjectivities, experiences and embodiments. My earlier research (2007), for example, indicated the ways in which working environments enable – and disable – possibilities of identity presentation. Participants working in artistic and cultural industries were, overall, less concerned with normative gender presentation – or 'passing' – as were participants working in more 'traditional' occupations. At first reading, this was unrelated to social class or economic privilege, as concerns over 'fitting in' as a woman or as a man were felt by participants across a range of occupations – from bus driver to government advisor. However the impacts of 'not fitting in' were deeply classed. In this way, working class participants were much more likely to talk about hostile working environments, and those in precarious working environments were much more fearful of losing their jobs as a result of their transition. Subsequently, these participants often left it quite late in life before transition, indicating the intersections between class, gender and embodiment. My later research similarly found that differing levels of social capital affected levels of esteem – with middle class participants more likely to talk about 'knowing their rights', 'having recourse' and being 'backed up by law'. Both research projects found that social class had deep effects on lived environments, with those participants who lived in social housing speaking much more about the effects of living in transphobic and, sometimes violent, neighbourhoods. This is not to argue that middle-class spaces are more progressive – while middle-class values that stress 'politeness' and 'tolerance' may make prejudice less overt, it is no less pernicious – but to be mindful of the different spatial dimensions, and the impacts of such, that social class enacts.

A very clear, and firm, indicator of the link between the economic and the cultural in relation to issues of gender diversity arises in relation to embodiment. Participants in each of my research projects who wanted gender reassignment surgery spoke about the extended length of time they had to wait to see a gender specialist. Further, standards of care require that transgender people 'live in role' for two years before surgery is permitted on the National Health Service, which, once approved, can mean another extended waiting time before procedures begin. For many participants, the clear distinction between their gender identity and gendered presentation was deeply distressing and, moreover, decreased their levels of personal safety. Participants also spoke of these issues in terms of their negative impacts on relationships with family, children, partners, lovers and friends. Accordingly, participants with economic resources were able to bypass these systemic failures by travelling abroad for surgery or by paying for private medical treatment in the United Kingdom.

Each of these examples indicates the ways in which the economic and the cultural cannot be separated in an analysis of transgender identities, embodiments and rights. Moreover, identities and subjectivities related to race and ethnicity rub alongside those discussed above – gender, sexuality, class, age and embodiment – among others, to produce distinct experiences and affects. An intersectional analysis, however, runs counter to recognition theory, which insists on demarcating economic and cultural instances of recognition. Further, recognition theory adopts a deductive view of the material, conceptualising materiality largely in terms of economic resources. This leaves embodiment – the materiality of the body – which is crucial for analysing transgender rights, hanging; the body is neither 'here' – material/redistribution – or 'there' – cultural/recognition. Rather, embodiment belongs firmly to both arenas at both theoretical and political levels.

My second key critique of recognition theory and politics concerns the essentialising of identities.

Essentialising identities and notions of universalism

Throughout the chapters of this book, the problematics of essentialising identities within recognition politics has been a recurring theme. This was recognised by Fraser (1997) in her discussion of identity politics, as discussed in Chapters 1 and 2; hence marginalised subjects seek recognition, or, to use Honneth's (1995) term, esteem, through collective organisation and articulation. Clearly, all political moments are collective moments, which turn on instances – and expressions – of recognition. Problems arise, however, when collective recognition is produced through opposition – though not difference – to others. Such moments thus lead to the construction of identity border – building, which, in turn, is monitored and regulated. Examples of the ways in which trans people have been subject to processes of exclusion were drawn out in Chapter 3 – first in relation to the ways that sexual social movements distanced themselves from trans people in the 1970s and then in terms of the ways in which trans men and women were rejected by some feminist and lesbian communities in the 1980s and 1990s. Moreover, although some contemporary feminist cultures, and particularly those of young feminist women and men, have worked to build bridges with trans communities, other high-profile feminist individuals and campaigns retain an explicit anti-transgender stance. Thus the subject of the relationship between feminism and transgender has long been debated and remains contentious (see Hines, 2004).

Yet, the pitfalls of identity politics also emerge within marginalised communities themselves. Hence, as I discussed in Chapter 4, my earlier research found that identity conflicts based around notions of (trans) gendered authenticity were apparent within transgender communities. The effects of battles around identity and community membership are most detrimental to the most marginalised group members who, as I explored in different ways across Chapters 4–6, are unable or unwilling to confirm to normalising strategies. As discussed, in terms of transgender, this appears in a politics of embodiment where expectations of normative gendered bodily presentation – from outside and within trans communities – often work to discriminate against those who present and/or identify outside of a male/female binary. Thus the body becomes a site of identity contestation and regulation.

The empirical research that has been drawn on throughout the book indicates that the passing of the UK GRA and CPA in 2004 not only represents significant shifts in social, cultural and legal understandings of, and practices towards, gender and sexual diversity – which, in turn, impact significantly upon experiences of citizenship – but also marks a key moment of transformation within gender and sexual politics. In this way, research participants often spoke about the GRA as representing a split in the 'trans movement'. Younger activists in particular were deeply critical of what, in their view, were comprises made by the campaigning organisations who worked alongside the government in the drafting of legislation. Such comprises were made in order to lessen political controversy (around, for example, 'gay marriage' and non-normative gender presentation) in order to smooth the passing of legislation through parliament. Research indicates that in a post GRA and CPA climate, political activism is increasingly being organised against notions of rights and recognition and that many activists are deeply critical about comprises to be made in claiming citizenship.

Discourses of essentialism – and their underpinning of 'sameness' – however, do not only operate at the levels of collective politics and social movement organisation. In this way, Chapter 3 explored how notions of universalism underpin European legal recognition frameworks and local (United Kingdom) law and policy. As discussed, universalist assumptions construct citizens along racialised, as well as gendered and sexualised, lines, working to reinforce and reproduce inequalities. Chapter 5 examined the arguments of a number of scholars who have been critical of the ways in which universalist assumptions construct discourses and practices of citizenship. Political theorists have made similar points in relation to the limits of liberal thinking. As Iris Marion Young argues, 'Modern normative reason and its political expression in the idea of the civic public, then, attain unity and coherence through the expulsion and confinement of everything that would threaten to invade the polity with differentiation' (1990: 111). These points were also apparent in Chapter 5 in relation to the regulation of practices of intimacy and sexuality. Here an essentialist discourse confers citizenship status on the basis of normalised sexual and intimate practices, while other ways of living personal lives are penalised; the divorce clause in the GRA acts as a clear example.

My third key critique of recognition theory and politics relates to the production of afflicted narratives.

Narratives of loss and suffering

As discussed in Chapter 1, Axel Honneth (1995) suggests that recognition politics emerges from a fundamental urge to avoid the 'moral suffering' that results from misrecognition. Similarly, Charles Taylor (1995) identifies the oppressing and imprisoning effects of misrecognition. From this perspective, recognition is *the* route beyond the detrimental impacts of misrecognition or non-recognition. Narratives of loss and suffering thus become narratives of respect and esteem. Yet, other scholars have developed more critical responses. For Lauren Berlant (2000) and Wendy Brown (2000), for example, recognition narratives do not represent triumphs over adversity, rather they characterise the sentimentalisation of loss. As Lois McNay writes, 'far from being authentic indicators of oppression or injustice, recognition claims derive their legitimacy from a certain sentimentalized discourse of suffering' (2008: 10).

There are connections here to Ken Plummer's (1995) work on the telling of sexual stories in which Plummer explores how certain stories are able to be told – and heard – at particular moments, while others cannot. Thus the 'coming out' narrative is a story which resounds with broader social, cultural, legal and policy shifts in relation to homosexuality and, as such, the story teller has a willing audience: 'stories of private, pathological pain have become stories of public, political participation' (Plummer, 1995). Yet, other sexual stories, for example, around inter-generational sex, rub up too closely against current cultural anxieties and, accordingly, do not have a voice. Although from a different premise – one which seeks to make discourse theory more applicable for understanding embodied social identity – Selya Benhabib (1999) also problematises the authentication of narrative. Thus Benhabib suggests that the 'truth' of the story, or even its content, is not what matters. What is significant is 'one's ability to keep telling a story about who one is that makes sense to oneself and to others' (Benhabib, 1999: 347).

The contextualisation of narrative troubles the notion that loss narratives speak to authentic or essential emotions. This is not to deny their validity, but rather to recognise the ways in which experience itself is socially mediated. Joan Scott's (1992) work on the problems of using experience as evidence is central here. Scott calls into question the ways in which 'experience' is utilised to naturalise discursively produced identities. In turn, she argues, this overgeneralises group differences. Scott's points here resound with discussions of authenticity and universalism above. Further, as McNay points out, such narratives run counter to collectivity: 'This rhetoric of personal pain is the internalised effect of a certain type of neo-liberal regulation that depoliticises oppression by establishing a universal equivalence of individual suffering' (McNay, 2008: 10). In her work on gender and class, Beverley Skeggs (2011) accordingly suggests that a politics of recognition is, on the whole, a middle-class politics as it is largely privileged groups whose outlook enables them to turn suffering to their benefit and self-improvement.

Skegg's argument about privilege links firmly to considerations of agency, which inform my fourth key point of critique of recognition theory and politics.

Power and agency

Recognition theory has a complicated relationship to questions of power and agency. As I discussed in Chapter 1, the notion of identity is at the crux of recognition politics and theory. The meanings and significance of identity – and, as discussed above, their intersections with other identities – are never fleshed out in the recognition literature. Rather, identity stands as the all pervading yet translucent mode of being. This leaves the distinctions between individual and collective identities underexplored (McNay, 2008) and fails to account for the relationship between identity and subjectivity. McNay illustrates this with reference to gender:

> Gender oppression, for example, is misunderstood by being construed as, in its essence, a form of interpersonally engendered misrecognition rather than also as systematically generated oppression. This is not to deny that inequalities are created through personal interaction, but, by focusing principally on this mode, the idea of recognition obscures the extent to which identity and subjectivity are penetrated by structural dynamics of power, which operate at one remove from the immediate relations of everyday life.
>
> McNay (2008: 9)

As discussed in Chapter 1, a model of recognition pays attention to political processes that are created outside of structural procedures. Subsequently, a politics of recognition talks of the motivating factors of emotions: respect, esteem and love. In this way, recognition theory could be read as a political theory of affect. Yet, as discussed above, affects are too often conceptualised as essential, naturalised motivators. This leaves the structuralising forces of the emotions of recognition unaccounted for. As McNay argues:

> The naturalized model of agency that this ensures is predicated on a one-way causality in which psychological dynamics determine social patterns of behaviour. This forecloses, *inter alia*, any but the most limited understanding of the way in which social forces might be understood as having conditioning effects upon the psyche. Instead of viewing the need for recognition as an inherent part of the human psychology, for example, it might be understood as an ideological construction.
>
> McNay (2008: 10)

These points of critique link back to the themes discussed about the construction of recognition narratives. If 'moments' (or stories) of recognition are read as ideologically constructed, the next step is to consider the processes and sources of construction. Still, it is impossible to pinpoint *the* instance of recognition. As I discussed in the Introduction to this book, the moment of recognition of gender diversity – and of gender diverse people – in the West is nebulous: it could be fixed at the turn of the 19th Century in sexology, or it may have occurred with the increase of surgical technologies in the 1950s. On the other hand, it might be located in the 1960s around the time of the Stonewall Riots, or, alternatively, arisen in the 1990s through the birth of transgender studies. Then again, it may well (in the United Kingdom and Portugal) be placed in August 2004 when Nadia Almada won the public vote as winner in the UK reality TV show *Big Brother.* But perhaps it happened in the late 1990s in the ECHR. Or it possibly took shape in April 2005 when the UK GRA came into effect. Of course, the recognition of certain aspects of gender diversity transpired across these moments – and many more besides. The point is, then, that particular moments of recognition are intrinsically linked to certain social, cultural and economic epochs. In this way, Chapter 5 drew out the ways that the acceptance of 'gay marriage' could be tied to times of austerity, while Chapter 6 traced (trans) gender and sexual recognition to neo-liberal processes of assimilation. Moreover, Chapters 4–6 explored how particular conditions of recognition construct specific subjects as being worthy of citizenship – at the expense of groups who remain misrecognised or are non-recognised anew. And, as previous chapters have addressed, the structural construction of the deserving/undeserving subject then plays out within marginalised communities themselves, working to further disempower the disenfranchised. To return to the work of Lois McNay:

> the desire for recognition might be far from a spontaneous and innate phenomenon but the effect of certain ideological manipulation of individuals. Such a critical perspective is foregone by thinkers who naturalize the idea of recognition by failing to examine more thoroughly the way in which emotions and other aspects of embodied subjectivity are mediated through social relations of power.
>
> McNay (2008: 10–11)

With these points in mind, the notion of a primordial drive to recognition, as apparent in the recognition literature considered in

Chapter 1, appears naïve. While theories of recognition can, at first glance, be seen to grant agency to subordinated groups through narrating a journey from loss to liberation, this trajectory can only be arrived at if power relations remain untheorised. An understanding of agency that is arrived at through negating the weight of structural and discursive (material and cultural) forces of power ultimately works to individualise and, as such, undermine the notion of the agentic subject in recognition theory.

In this section of the chapter, I have set out four key critiques of recognition theory and politics as they have related to central themes across the chapters of this book. These relate to the essentialising of identity and discourses of universalism, the construction of narratives of loss and suffering, a lack of intersectional analysis and the under-theorisation of power and agency. In each of these ways, a theory and politics of recognition is, in my view, an unproductive framework for the theorisation of gender and sexual diversity. In the following section, I explore Iris Marion Young's work on a politics of difference. This is evaluated to consider the extent to which a politics of difference may overcome the problems with recognition at both conceptual and political levels that I have explored here.

Iris Marion Young's politics of difference

Five faces of oppression

Iris Marion Young's intervention to the recognition literature was considered at various points in Chapter 1. Here I turn to examine in detail her notion of a politics of difference. Young's contribution to recognition debates speaks to the problems with theory and politics of recognition that I have discussed above. More broadly, her critique resonates with the concerns around an undifferentiated liberal model of social justice that were first raised in Chapter 1, but have surfaced in different ways through each of the subsequent chapters of this book.

In *Justice and the Politics of Difference* Young (1990) examines the implications for political philosophy – and, especially, for questions of social justice – of the claims of social movements around race and ethnicity, gender and sexuality. Young's starting point, as was discussed in Chapter 1, is that rather than beginning by focusing on distribution, understandings of justice need to begin with the concepts of domination and oppression. The origin of Young's thesis, thus, foregrounds issues of power; attending from the start to the issue of an under-theorisation of power within recognition theory as discussed above. Young distinguishes between five 'faces' of oppression. The first three categories relate to the social division of labour under Capitalism: exploitation – the transference of the results of the labour of one social group to benefit another; marginalisation – the groups the system of labour does not use; powerlessness – lack of authority, status and sense of self (which particularly is attached to professionalism). These three categories, Young argues, are structural and institutional facets of oppression; they are the:

> relations that delimit people's material lives, including, but not restricted to the resources they have access to and the concrete opportunities that they have or do not have to develop and exercise their capacities. These kinds of oppression are a matter of concrete power in relation to others – of who benefits from whom, and who is dispensable.
>
> Young (1990: 58)

The last two categories are: cultural imperialism – whereby the dominant meanings of society silence the perspective of another, and stereotype and mark out a group as Other; and violence – the physical and psychological effects of attacks on people or their property. Importantly, these criteria account for the material (redistribution), cultural (recognition) and those across and between redistribution and recognition.

The presence of any of these five conditions, Young suggests, is enough to determine whether a group is oppressed. Moreover, different groups show different combinations of each, as do different individuals in groups:

> Nearly all, if not all, groups said by contemporary social movements to be oppressed suffer cultural imperialism. The other oppressions they experience vary. Working-class people are exploited and powerless, for example, but if employed and white, do not experience marginalization and violence. Gay men, on the other hand, are not just gay exploited or powerless, but they experience severe cultural imperialism and violence. Similarly,

> Jews and Arabs as groups are victims of cultural imperialism and violence though many members of these groups also suffer exploitation or powerlessness. Old people are oppressed by marginalization and cultural imperialism, and this is also true of physically and mentally disabled people. As a group women are subject to gender-based exploitation, powerlessness, cultural imperialism, and violence. Racism in the United States condemns many Blacks and Latinos to marginalization, and puts many more at risk, even though many members of these groups escape that condition; members of these groups often suffer all five forms of oppression.
>
> Young (1990: 64)

Young's 'five faces' model enables exploration of different forms of oppressions (within and across groups) without operating on a hierarchical basis. Moreover, this model is attuned to distinct features of oppression or, to use Young's phrase, 'intensity of those oppressions' (1990: 65). Here, Young speaks to the importance of intersectionality across and within social groups; thus tending to the lack of intersectional analysis in recognition theory as discussed above. Young's model of oppression also speaks, though not directly, to the concerns set out above about recognition's rehearsal of a narrative of loss and suffering. Thus while Young does, indeed, speak of suffering – of the pains of oppression – she links such affects strongly to both structural and discursive systems of power. Young's oppressed subjects are, then, always agentic subjects.

Thus far in my evaluation of Iris Marion Young's model of social justice, I have suggested that her thesis remedies that which is lacking in relation to three of my four key points of critique of recognition theory as discussed in the preceding section of this chapter: the under-theorisation of issues of power and agency; narratives of loss and suffering; and intersectionality. In these ways, Young provides a set of theoretical tools for an analysis of gender and sexual diversity. First it can be used to think about the ways in which inequalities of gender and sexual diversity are both material and cultural; second it provides a means through which to explore intersecting axes of inequality across, between and within gender and sexual social movements; third it can be utilised to theorise the structural and discursive systems that not only construct unequal power relations for gender and sexually diverse groups but also work to bring those groups into being, in and of themselves, in the first instance. Each of these points has emerged in and across the preceding chapters of this book and, in each instance, recognition theory and politics, is, I have suggested, limited in its ability to fully account for these issues. In what follows, the chapter considers the ways in which Young critically responds to the problems of identity essentialisation and to notions of universalism that have also figured large in my critique of recognition theory and politics in this and earlier chapters of the book.

Affirming difference

A key critique running through this book and summarised in the previous section of this chapter is that recognition theory and politics – and consideration of both facets individually is important here – theorise identities as universal. I have, throughout the book, spoken about this in different ways. In Chapter 1, I critiqued recognition theory for essentialising identity categories. My use of the term essentialism was apparent also in Chapter 2 when I looked at the ways in which gender diverse people have, historically, been excluded from gender and sexual social movements, which sought recognition on the basis of rigid definitions of gender and sexuality. In Chapter 3, I invoked the notion of universalism to address the ways in which human rights law configured fixed notions of gender and sexual identity, which, while working productively for some, discriminated further against others. These themes were drawn out further in Chapters 4–6, which also employed the term 'sameness' to address how UK law and policy, and frameworks of equality and diversity, have institutionalised particular routes of, and means to, inclusion. These practices, I suggested, were especially apparent through debates around citizenship and governance, and, in each instance, I argued that processes of normalisation worked to dilute diversity. Though criticisms of, and challenges to, discourses and practices of 'sameness' are strong throughout transgender theory, queer theory and critical branches of sexuality studies, critical race studies, postcolonial studies, political theory and gender studies, few scholars have moved on from the level of critique to that of resolve. It is here, then, at the levels of analysis and resolution that Iris Marion Young's work is particularly salient.

Running through the recognition literature is the liberal idea that social differentiation – in other words, inequality – would cease if social groups were treated equally. Within this model of social justice, 'difference' and 'differentiation' are accredited the same negative connotations. Hence 'sameness' works to equalise. Young refutes this recognition thesis, arguing instead that egalitarian politics requires the affirmation of difference – that which she terms a politics of difference:

> In this version, the good society does not eliminate or transcend group difference. Rather, there is equality among social and culturally differentiated groups, who mutually respect one another and affirm one another in their differences.
>
> Young (1990: 163)

This model of social justice – or version of the good society – stands at odds with rights-based claims founded on notions of assimilationism and is in stark contrast to neoliberal understandings of equality and diversity. The denouncement of difference has different political underpinnings; it may be articulated as a call for collectivism from the Left or as denial of inequality from the Right. Yet, regardless of on which side of the political fence the equality narrative is told, the same outcomes – what Young terms 'oppressive consequences' (1990: 164) – occur. First, Young argues, 'blindness to difference' further disadvantages groups 'whose experience, culture, and socialized capacities differ from those of privileged groups' (1990: 164):

> So assimilationism always implies coming into the game after it is already begun, after the rules and the standards have already been set, and having to prove oneself according to those rules. In the assimilationist strategy, the privileged groups implicitly define the standards according to which all will be measured.
>
> Young (1990: 164)

At various points, this book has drawn on empirical material that has illustrated the workings of this. My research findings have thus indicated the ways in which assimilationist strategies – both external (from legal and policy frameworks, from medical practitioners, from workplaces) and internal (from identity politics within gender and sexual communities) – benefit those willing or able to assimilate and further disadvantage those who cannot or will not live by normative standards of gender and sexual expression.

Young's second critique of a politics that is 'blind' to difference is that the notions of universalism enable the most privileged groups to ignore their own group specificity. Thus:

> allowing norms expressing the point of view and experiences of the privileged groups to appear neutral and universal [. . .] Against a supposedly neutral humanist ideal, only the oppressed groups come to be marked with particularity; they, and not the privileged groups, are marked, objectified as the Others.
>
> Young (1990: 165)

Resonating here is the recent development of the term 'cisgendered' by transgender theorists and activists who, in affirmation of difference, have sought to speak of non-trans people, not only trans people, as a gendered group. Similar developments are evident with the emergence of critical white studies, which speaks of 'whiteness' as a racialised group, bringing to light, and calling into question, this category's neutrality and privilege.

Young's third point of contention is that a 'difference blind' politics leads to the internal devaluation of difference by group members themselves:

> When there is an ideal of general human standards according to which everyone should be evaluated equally, then Puerto Ricans or Chinese Americans are ashamed of their accents or their parents. Black children despise the female dominated kith and kin networks of their neighbourhoods, and feminists seek to root out their tendency to cry, or to feel compassion for a frustrated stranger. The aspiration to assimilate helps produce the self-loathing and the double consciousness characteristic of oppression. The goal of assimilation holds up to people a demand that they 'fit', be like the mainstream, in behaviour, values, and goals.
>
> Young (1990: 165)

A central theme of this book has been the closing down of gender and sexual difference at the levels of the subjective and the embodied. Thus, at different moments in preceding chapters, I have argued that the UK GRA enables gender and sexual diversity only at the levels that they cease to become diverse. Accordingly, trans people are granted recognition if they fit with prevailing norms of binary gender formation (male/female) and dominant notions of gendered intimacy (homo/hetero). The empirical research, drawn on in these instances, indicates the ways in which trans people often feel pressurised to fit these categories or are forced to forgo the rights of recognition. Moreover, such pressures to conform – to 'pass' – are internalised and, as such, bleed into community politics around identity and belonging. Yet, as Chapter 5 suggested, some sections of gendered and sexual social movements are vocal in their refusal to assimilate – to present as men or as women, to divorce or to marry. What I termed here moments of non-recognition, Iris Marion Young would characterise, and celebrate, as instances of a politics of difference. Of such, Young says:

> In the act of reclaiming the identity the dominant culture has taught them to despise [...], and affirming it as an identity to celebrate, the oppressed remove the double consciousness. I am just what they say I am – a Jewboy, a colored girl, a fag, a dyke, a hag – and proud of it. No longer does one have the impossible project of trying to become something one is not under circumstances where the very trying reminds one of who one is.
>
> Young (1990: 166)

A positive focus on 'difference' is central to queer theory. Yet a lack of material and embodied analysis within queer theory has been problematic for analysing transgender experience (Hines, 2006a, 2007a). Young's points of argument here suggest how a politics of difference may be utilised to overcome the limitations of 'queer' while, at the same time, retaining queer theory's non-essentialising tendencies. In this way, Young's argument is similar to what, elsewhere, I have termed a 'sociological queer theory' (Hines, 2007a). Thus difference is commemorated within a material analysis. Further, a politics of differences enables alliances and allegiances to be made across communities:

> In our complex, plural society, every social group has group differences cutting across it, which are potential sources of wisdom, excitement, conflict and oppression. Gay men, for example, may be Black, rich, homeless, or old, and these differences produce different identifications and potential conflicts among gay men, as well as affinities with some straight men.
>
> Young (1990: 172–173)

A major strength of Young's argument in this passage, to my mind, is her inclusion of identity conflict alongside the more, oft cited, positive tenets of difference – for example, within queer studies. Unlike the negation of difference from either the Left or the Right, as discussed above, Young is not claiming that 'sameness' is something that is, or can be, realised. But neither is she claiming that difference is always easy. At the start of this section, I suggested that Young was among the few social theorists to not only productively conceptualise difference but to also develop a political model to account for difference. Another exception is Steven Seidman, who remarks 'Indeed, I wonder whether at least some of the resistance to pragmatism reflects a fear of living with differences that "run deep"' (1997: 258). Seidman continues:

> In such a society as the contemporary US, where differences have crystallized into sociocultural differences and where conventions of discourse – styles, logics, categories, epistemologies – are regularly contested, a pragmatic culture of reason that is respectful of difference, comfortable with ambiguity, and orientated toward inventiveness and temporary agreements would seem especially appropriate, encouraging civil, peaceful, democratic modes of managing collective life.
>
> Seidman (1997: 264–265)

Seidman's affirmation of difference leads him to conceptualising a politics of pragmatism. Young's affirmation of difference leads her to argue for its inclusion in policy. Hence she proposes a rethinking of liberal citizenship, calling instead for the pluralisation of the citizenship 'ideal'. In later work, she argues that such an ideal can only be incorporated into policy if policy makers ensure that minority groups are fully encouraged by public bodies to take part in dialogue: 'the perception of anything like public good can only be an outcome of public interaction that expresses rather than submerges particularities' (Young, 2000: 119). To these ends, she states the need for law and policy makers to actively consult with minority groups when developing law or policies that affect their members.

Conclusion

This chapter, the last chapter of this book, has looked back across preceding chapters to summarise my key points of critique of a theory and politics of recognition. This chapter thus began by offering a précis of my key points of critique. These arose in relation to a lack of attention to intersectionality; the essentialisation of identity and notions of universalism; the construction of narratives of loss and suffering; and the under-theorisation of power and agency. In exploring each of these limits of recognition theory and politics, together, this section of the chapter served to hone my argument as to recognition's limits for a theory and politics of gender and sexual diversity as it developed throughout the previous chapters of the book.

The chapter moved on to examine Iris Marion Young's theory of a politics of difference. In looking at Young's model for social justice in depth, I sought to indicate how a politics of difference may be seen to remedy the limitations with a theory and politics of recognition. A politics of difference, framework, I suggested, holds much greater potential for enabling social justice in relation to gender and sexual diversity than does the notion of recognition at either the conceptual or the political level. The closing section of the chapter considered Young's ideas on how a politics of difference might be applied to law and policy. Here I outlined Young's proposals for increased consultation and interaction with constituent members. These points are central to the premise of this book and are explored in relation to my own research in the concluding chapter.

Conclusion

The first section of the conclusion presents a summary of the findings from my research project 'Gender Diversity, Recognition and Citizenship'. The research objectives, design and questions were established in the book's Introduction, and findings from the project have been drawn upon throughout the seven chapters. The Conclusion then outlines the recommendations drawn from this research. The next section summarises the key arguments of each of the chapters in the book and offers a final consideration of the significance of a politics of difference for accounting for gender and sexual diversity. The final section of this chapter returns to Iris Marion Young's thoughts on implementing difference through policy, which were discussed at the close of Chapter 7. I argue for the importance of knowledge sharing and knowledge exchange initiatives in order to implement these principles.

Summary of research findings

Overall, participants in the project 'Gender Diversity, Recognition and Citizenship' felt that the UK GRA (2004) was an important and significant law in terms of transgendered equality legislation. The majority of participants had registered, planned to register or wished to register (though were restricted by the criteria) for a GRC under the law. A minority of participants actively did not want to register.

The significance of the Act was, in the main, linked pragmatically to the changing of documents and, in this way, was, largely, discussed strategically rather than as a subjective reflection of gender identity. The GRA was seen to have had little impact on relationships with family or friends or at work. It was hoped that the Act would have a positive social and cultural impact regarding transgender people, although the link between law and broader societal attitudes was sometimes disputed. While some participants had found the process of recognition straightforward, others had found it a complex and problematic procedure, particularly in relation to the required evidence from GPs and psychiatrists.

That the Act did not require surgery was overwhelmingly viewed positively, although the continued role of psychiatrists in the gender recognition process was strongly criticised by many participants. The GRA also came under criticism for neglecting the rights of non-gendered people. While a minority of participants felt directly excluded from the new rights brought by the GRA in this respect, a larger group felt that they were inappropriately forced to fit into categories of male or female. In this way, the GRA was critiqued for reproducing a binary gender model. The divorce criteria in the GRA came under much criticism. While a group of participants had benefitted from the Act as they were now able to marry in their acquired gender, participants who remained married to their pre-transition partners spoke angrily about having to choose between marriage to their long-standing partners and gender recognition. While it was felt that civil partnerships worked for transgender people who were in same-sex relationships, linking the CPA and the GRA, as the Government had done in defence of the divorce clause, showed a lack of understanding of the complex relationship between gender and sexuality.

Overall, the project found that the UK GRA was seen to be an important first step towards greater equality for transgender people; a stepping-stone to full citizenship rights; as Fleur said: 'the GRA is a good start, but there is much more to be done' (Fleur, age 51).

Research recommendations

Research findings suggest that the following moves are needed to secure that all transgender people obtain the same levels of recognition and protection under the GRA:

1. The removal of 'gender dysphoria' from the DSM
2. A simplified application process and less requirement of medical evidence

3. An end to the involvement of psychiatric practitioners in the legal process of gender recognition
4. Recognition for non-gendered and multi-gendered people
5. The removal of the divorce clause

Like the key findings, the research recommendations speak to concerns and matters of debate as they have arisen across the chapters of this book.

Chapter conclusions

Chapter 1 began by considering the role of recognition in social movement activism. A political theory of recognition developed to account for the rise of new social movements that organised around issues of identity and difference, culture and community. The chapter then looked in more detail at the principles of recognition as they are addressed in the work of Axel Honneth (1995), Charles Taylor (1995) and Nancy Fraser (1995), paying particular attention to modes of respect and esteem and to debates around redistribution/recognition. Employing research data, the chapter also considered what recognition meant to participants. Research narratives often resonated with the themes of respect and esteem that run through the recognition literature. Moreover, a central point that was articulated in favour of the GRA related to moving beyond a diagnosis, and social perception, of mental illness. Yet, as the chapter indicated, the criteria for gender recognition remains tied to a medical model of transgender, to which the notion of 'gender dysphoria' is central. It was from this premise that the research arrived at its first recommendation: the removal of gender dysphoria from the DSM, the guidebook for mental health professionals on diagnosing and treating mental illness.

In the latter section of Chapter 1, I suggested that transgender recognition claims are made at both the levels of the material (redistributive) and recognition (cultural). Drawing on the work of Iris Marion Young (1997) and Judith Butler (1998), I thus argued for an intersectional analysis of the economic and the cultural. Chapter 2 developed this argument further by drawing on substantive material to further explore the role of recognition to social movement politics around gender and sexuality. In charting the rise of these new social movements in the late 1960s, I argued that collective politics has not only brought about legal and policy changes, but has increased the social and cultural visibility of non-normative gender and sexual practices and identities. Again, I emphasised the ways in which these politics were both material and cultural. Chapter 2 moved on to consider the intrinsic, and problematic, relationship of identity politics to recognition theory. As I illustrated, there is a long history of trans people's exclusion from gender and sexuality movements because of a politics of identity that serves to regulate community belonging through recourse to essential categories (of man/woman; homo/hetero).

Chapter 3 linked domestic law and politics to those at a European level; highlighting several cases that were taken to the ECHR by trans people who argued that British law, as it stood, discriminated against the rights of trans people, particularly in relation to the right to privacy, to a family life and to marry. These cases, I suggested, formed the backdrop to the 2004 UK GRA. Yet, as I explored, universalist notions of identity and rights hamper the protection of gender and sexuality diversity. In critiquing the notion of universalism in human rights and recognition discourses and practices, the chapter drew on a range of literatures: feminist theory, sexuality studies, post-colonial and queer literatures, to highlight significant problems with universalism and Western-based politics of recognition. These issues were further developed in Chapter 4, which drew on empirical data to explore a range of experiences of the GRA for research participants. While some participants articulated positive accounts of gaining gender recognition, many others found the process problematic. In particular, the evidence required by the Panel was deemed inappropriate and, or, difficult to secure. From this, the research drew its second recommendation: a simplified application process and less requirement of medical evidence.

Chapter 4 indicated the ways in which the GRA was subject to further critique from research participants. First, the primary role of psychiatrists in the gender recognition process, as members of the Gender Recognition Panel, was challenged by the majority of participants, who argued for the least possible intervention by medical practitioners in the formal process of recognition. Second, research findings indicated that strong critiques were brought to bear on the GRA for its lack of provision for non-gendered people. With these points in mind, the research developed its third and fourth recommendations: an end to the involvement of psychiatric practitioners in the legal process of gender recognition; and recognition for non-gendered and multi-gendered people.

Chapter 5 turned to practices of intimate diversity. Here I explored the ways in which recent legislative shifts such as the UK GRA (GRA, 2004) and the UK CPA (2004) both supported and worked against practices of intimate diversity. A range of literature on intimate and sexual identities and practices was drawn upon here to evaluate claims for intimate recognition – particularly that of marriage. While research findings found that some participants had benefitted from the GRA in that they were now able to marry in their acquired gender, others – most notably, those who remained married to pre-transition partners – found their intimate lives further regulated; they were forced to choose between gender and partnership recognition. Research participants overwhelmingly spoke out against the demand that an applicant for gender recognition has to first divorce. Correspondingly, the research developed its fifth recommendation: removal of the divorce clause.

In Chapter 6, I contextualised the UK GRA within a raft of UK equality and diversity law and policy around gender and sexuality. The chapter first considered the ways in which concepts central to recognition politics such as 'equality', 'diversity' and 'citizenship' became articulated in relation to gender and sexuality, first by UK's New Labour Government, and then, more recently, by the Conservative/Liberal Democratic Coalition Government. Central to the arguments of this chapter is the utilisation of 'sameness', which, I suggested, works to guide normalising discourse and practices. These issues were drawn out further as the chapter addressed debates around citizenship and assimilation. The chapter then drew on recent conceptual and empirical studies examining the ways in which UK equality and diversity policy has been institutionalised and implemented. These were applied alongside my own research findings to evaluate diversity's success. My argument here was that 'diversity' is frequently weakened through its institutionalisation. Moreover, legal and policy shifts around gender and sexuality were seen to produce dichotomous frameworks, which strengthened traditional hierarchies, while bringing new inequalities into being. Towards the end of this chapter, I thus argued that new forms of gendered and sexuality inequality are patterned through an equality and diversity drive.

From this juncture, Chapter 7 drew on Iris Marion Young's (1990) model of a 'politics of difference'. This followed a summary of my key points of critique of recognition theory and politics as they have been developed through the preceding chapters of the book: the lack of an intersectional analysis; the essentialisation and universalism of identity; the construction of narratives of loss and suffering; and the under-theorisation of power and agency. Subsequently, I suggested that Young's model of social justice – that of a politics of difference – had the potential to overcome the limits of recognition theory and politics. Thus, I outlined the ways in which each element in her model of the 'five faces of oppression' was beneficial to theorising gender and sexual diversity. At this stage I wish to return to the point at which Chapter 7 closed: to Young's proposals for applying difference in, and through, policy.

Exchanging knowledge

Iris Marion Young's model of a politics of difference is not only significant at conceptual and political levels but also important in its consideration of how to implement these ideas (and ideals) at policy levels. Young's work, then, is a valuable example of praxis. From this premise, I wish to think about a politics of difference as a way of *doing* difference. Reflecting back on her earlier work on the theorisation of social justice, Young (2000) discusses the importance of dialogue between policy makers and public bodies, and minority groups. The onus is on the former organisations to ensure public interaction. I add to this the value of, and the need for, increased interaction and dialogue between academics and community groups – between the researcher and the researched. Though much has been done in the social sciences to improve these levels of communication, most research remains in the academy and, accordingly, has little impact on stakeholder groups and concerned individuals. It is important to break this tradition and to fracture still the current divide between academic and non-academic communities. Collaboration between participants and researchers in knowledge sharing and exchange is key here.[1] Alongside increased dialogue between policy makers, public bodies and marginalised communities, I propose that a commitment to 'public sociology'[2] is vital for the implementation of a politics of difference.

Moreover, a politics of difference requires that the motivator of these channels of communication is the expression – not the submergence – of particularity. As I have indicated at various points throughout this book, notions of 'sameness' run through recent equality and diversity frameworks and initiatives at legal and policy levels. Thus, while some members of minority groups benefit from increased recognition, many more remain on the borders of citizenship. As I have suggested, it is the most marginalised who become more disenfranchised. Occupying these borderlands is to occupy a state of misrecognition or non-recognition. Chapter 6 of this book evaluated the implementation of equality and diversity agendas across a number of spheres. In the main, these agendas were judged to have failed in relation to protecting the rights, and accounting for the needs, of members of minority groups. Such failings, I propose, arise from values of sameness and expectations of assimilation. I thus offer a politics of difference not only as a way of rethinking gender and sexual diversity in contemporary times but also as a method of, and a politics for, social change.

Notes

1. Reason and Bradbury's (2008) notion of 'participatory action research' is relevant here. Reason and Bradbury define this as research that is 'participative, grounded in experience, and action-oriented' (2008:xxiv).
2. Michael Burawoy (2004) distinguishes between 'public' and 'professional' sociology. The former is motivated by interaction with wider audiences outside academia, while the latter is concerned with addressing other professional sociologists.

References

Adam, B. (1992) 'Sex and Caring Among Men' in K. Plummer (ed.) *Modern Homosexualities: Fragments of Lesbian and Gay Experience*, London: Routledge: 175–183.

Ahmed, S. (2012) *On Being Included: Racism and Diversity in Institutional Life*, Durham: Duke University Press.

Allen, S., Sanders, L. and Wallis, J. (1974) *Contradictions of Illusion: Papers from the Women's Movement*, Leeds: Feminist Books.

Altman, D. (2001) *Global Sex*, Chicago, IL: The University of Chicago Press.

Appiah, Anthony K. (1994) 'Identity, Authenticity, Survival: Multicultural Societies and Social Reproduction' in Amy Gutmann (ed.) *Multiculturalism: Examining 'The Politics of Recognition'*, An essay by Charles Taylor, with commentary by K. Anthony Appiah, Jürgen Habermas, Steven C. Rockefeller, Michael Walzer, Susan Wolf, Princeton, NJ: Princeton University Press: 162–163.

Back, L. and Solomos, J. (2000) *Theories of Race and Racism: A Reader*, London: Routledge.

Barker, N. (2011) *Not the Marrying Kind: A Feminist Critique of Same-Sex Marriage*, Basingstoke: Palgrave Macmillan.

Barker, M. and Langdridge, D. (eds.) (2010) *Understanding Non-Monogamies, Routledge Research in Gender and Society*, Abingdon: Routledge.

Barry, B. (2001) *Culture and Equality: An Egalitarian Critique of Multiculturalism*, Cambridge: Polity.

Bauman, Z. (2003) , Cambridge: Polity Press.

Bawer, B. (1994) *Place at the Table: The Gay Individual in American Society*, New York: Touchstone.

Beck, U. and Beck-Gernsheim, E. (1995) *The Normal Chaos of Love*, Cambridge: Polity Press.

Bell, D. and Binnie, J. (2000) *The Sexual Citizen: Queer Politics and Beyond*, Cambridge: Polity Press.

Benhabib, S. (1999) 'Sexual Difference and Collective Identities: The New Global Constellation', *Signs*, 24 (2): 335–361.

Berlant, L. (2000) 'The Subject of True Feeling' in S. Ahmed, J. Kilby, C. Lury, M. McNeil and B. Skeggs (eds.) *Transformations: Thinking Through Feminism*, London: Routledge: 33–47.

Bindel, J. (2003) ' I changed for all the wrong reasons and then it was too late, *The Telegraph*. www.parakaleo.co.uk/article9.html (accessed January 2013).

Binnie, J. (2004) *The Globalisation of Sexuality*, London: Sage.

Binnie, J. and Klesse, C. (2011) 'Because it was a bit like going to an Adventure Park': The Politics of Hospitality in Transnational Lesbian, Gay, Bisexual, Transgender and Queer Activist Networks', *Journal of Tourism Consumption and Practice*, 11 (2): 154–170.

Bockting, W.O. and Coleman, E. (eds.) (1992) *Gender Dysphoria: Interdisciplinary Approaches in Clinical Management*, New York: The Haworth Press.
Bornstein, K. (1994) *Gender Outlaw: Men, Women and the Rest of Us*, New York: Routledge.
Boyd, N. A. (2006) 'Bodies in Motion: Lesbian and Transsexual Histories' in S. Stryker and S. Whittle (eds.) *The Transgender Studies Reader*, New York and Abingdon: Routledge: 420–433.
Brown, W. (2000) *States of Injury: Power and Freedom in Late Modernity*, Princeton: Princeton University Press.
Brown, G. (2007) 'Mutinous Eruptions: Autonomous Spaces of Radical Queer Activism', *Environment & Planning A*, 39 (11): 2685–2698.
Burawoy, M. (2004) *For Public Sociology*, American Sociological Association Conference Presidential Address.
Burns, C. (1998) 'Court Judgement Criticises UK Government's Lack of Action', Press for Change, http://www.pfc.org.uk/node/874, accessed March 2008.
Bussemaker, J. and Voet, R. (1998) 'Citizenship and Gender: Theoretical Approaches and Historical Legacies', *Critical Social Policy*, 18 (3): 278–307.
Butler, J. (1998) 'Merely Cultural', *New Left Review*, 227: 33–44.
Butler, J. (2004) *Undoing Gender*, New York: Routledge.
Califia, P. (1997) *Sex Changes: The Politics of Transgenderism*, San Francisco: Cleis Press.
Carrington, M. (2012) 'The Cultural Significance of Asexuality', http://markcarrigan.net/2012/01/31/the-cultural-significance-of-asexuality/, accessed January 2013.
Carter, D. (2004) *Stonewall: The Riots That Sparked The Gay Revolution*. New York: St. Martin's Press.
Casey, ME. (2007) Spatial (in)visibility and the Good Gay/Bad Gay Binary in G. Brown, K. Brown, J. Lim (eds.) *Geographies of Sexualities: Theory, Practice and Politics*, Aldershot: Ashgate: 125–136.
Castells, M. (1997) *The Information Age: Economy, Society and Culture. Volume 11: The Power of Identity*, Oxford: Blackwell.
Cobb (2012) *Single: Arguments for the Uncoupled*, New York: New York University Press.
Cohen, C. (2000) 'Punks, Bulldaggers, and Welfare Queens: The Radical Potential of Queer Politics?', *GLQ: A Journal of Lesbian and Gay Studies*, 3 (4): 437–65.
Connell, R.W. (1995) *Masculinities*, Cambridge: Polity Press.
Cooper, D. (1995) *Power in Struggle: Feminism, Sexuality and the State*, Buckingham: Open University Press.
Cooper, D. (2004) *Challenging Diversity: Rethinking Equality and the Value of Difference*, Cambridge: Cambridge University Press.
Cowan, S. (2005) 'Gender is no Substitute for Sex: A Comparative Human Rights Analysis of the Legal Regulation of Sexual Identity', *Feminist Legal Studies*, 13:67–96.

Cromwell, J. (1999) *Transmen and FTMs: Identities, Bodies, Genders and Sexualities*, Illinois: University of Illinois Press.

Davy, Z. (2011) *Recognizing Transsexuals: Personal, Political and Medicolegal Embodiment*, Farnham: Ashgate.

D'Emilio, J. (1983) *Sexual Politics, Sexual Communities*, Chicago: The University of Chicago Press.

D'Emilio, J. (2004) *The World Turned: Histories on Gay History, Politics and Culture*, Durham, NC: Duke University Press.

D'Emilio, J. and Freedman, E. (1988) *Intimate Matters: A History of Sexuality in America*, New York: Harper and Row.

Devor, H. (1989) *Gender Blending: Confronting the Limits of Duality*, Bloomington: Indiana University Press.

Devor, A. H. and Matte, N. (2006) 'One Inc. And Reed Erickson: The Uneasy Collaboration of Gay and Trans Activism, 1964–2003' in S. Stryker and S. Whittle (eds.) *The Transgender Studies Reader*, New York and Abingdon: Routledge: 387–406.

Duggan, L. (2002) *The Incredible Shrinking Public: Sexual Politics and the Decline of Democracy*, Boston, US: Beacon Press.

Dunne, G. (1999) 'A Passion for "Sameness" Sexuality and Gender Accountability' in E.B. Silva and C. Smart (eds.) *The New Family: The New Practices and Politics of Family Life*, London: Sage.

Duplessis, R.B. and Snitow, A. (1998) *The Feminist Memoir Project: Voices from Women's Liberation*, CA: Three Rivers Press.

Dwyer, P. (2004) *Understanding Social Citizenship: Issues for Policy and Practice*, First ed. Bristol: Policy Press.

Edelman, L. (2005) *No Future: Queer Theory and the Death Drive*, Durham, NC: Duke University Press.

Ekins, R. (1997) *Male Femaling: A Grounded Theory Approach to Cross-Dressing and Sex-Changing*, London and New York: Routledge.

Ekins, R. and King, D. (1996) *Blending Genders: Social Aspects of Cross-Dressing and Sex-Changing*, London: Routledge

Eng, D. L., Halberstam, J. and Monroz, J. (2005) 'Introduction: Special Issue What's Queer About Queer Studies Now?', *Social Text,* 23 (3/4): 84–5.

Epstein, S. (1999) 'Gay and Lesbian Movements in the United States: Dilemmas of Identity, Diversity and Political Strategy' in B. Adam, J. W Duyvendak and A. Krouwel (eds.) *The Global Emergence of Gay and Lesbian Politics: National Imprints of a Worldwide Movement*, Philadelphia: Temple University Press: 30–90.

Evans, D. (1993) *Sexual Citizenship: The Material Construction of Sexualities*, London: Lawrence & Wishart.

Fanon, F. (1952) *Black Skin, White Masks*, New York: Grove Press.

Feinberg, L. (1996) *Transgender Warriors: Making History From Joan of Arc to Dennis Rodman*, Boston: Beacon Press.

Follon and Sayers, (2011) https://sites.google.com/site/thinkingblack/home-1/equal-marriage, accessed February 2013.

Foucault, M. (1979) *The History of Sexuality, Volume 1: An Introduction*, London: Allen Lane.

Fraser, N. (1995) 'From Redistribution to Recognition? Dilemmas of Justice in a "Postsocialist" Age', *New Left Review*, 212: 68–93.

Fraser, N. (1997) *Justice Interruptus: Critical Reflections on the 'Postsocialist' Condition*, New York: Routledge.

Fraser, N. (2000) 'Rethinking Recognition' *New Left Review*, 3: 107–120.

Fraser, N. (2003) 'Rethinking Recognition: Overcoming Displacement and Reification in Cultural Politics' in B. Hobson (ed.) *Recognition Struggles and Social Movements: Contested Identities, Agency and Power*, Cambridge: Cambridge University Press: 21–34.

Fraser, N. (2008) *Scales of Justice*, Cambridge: Polity.

Freeman, J. (1971) 'The Revolution is Happening in our Minds' in J. Sochen (ed.) *The New Feminism in Twentieth Century America*, D. C: Heath and C0: 149–60.

French, T. (2013) 'Same-Sex Marriage Vote "Historic Day for Equality"', http://www.equalmarriage.org.uk/blog/, accessed February 2013.

Gedalof, I. (2013) 'Sameness and Difference in Government Equality Talk' in *Ethnic and Racial Studies,* Vol.36,: 1 pp.117–135.

Giddens, A. (1992) *The Transformation of Intimacy: Sexuality, Love and Eroticism in Modern Societies*, Cambridge: Polity Press.

Grabham, E. (2007) 'Citizen Bodies, Intersex Citizenship', *Sexualities*, 10 (1): 29–48.

Habermas, J. (1994) 'Struggles for Recognition in the Democratic Constitutional State' in A. Gutmann (ed.) *Multiculturalism: Examining the Politics of Recognition*, Princeton: Princeton University Press.

Halberstam, J. (1998) *Female Masculinity*, Durham: Duke University Press.

Halberstam, J. (2008) 'The Anti-Social Turn in Queer Studies', *Graduate Journal of Social Science: Queer Methodologies*, 5 (2): 104–56.

Hale, J. (1998) 'Tracing a Ghostly Memory in My Throat: Reflections of Ftm Feminist Voice and Agency' in T.Digby (ed.) *Men Doing Feminism*, New York and London: Routledge: 99–130.

Hall, S. (1990) 'Cultural Identity and Diaspora' in J. Rutherford (ed.) *Identity*, London: Lawrence & Wishart.: 222–237.

Haritaworn, J., Tauqir, T. and Erdemand, E. (2008) 'Gay Imperialism: The Role of Gender and Sexuality Discourses in the "War on Terror"' in E. Miyake and A. Kuntsman (eds.) *Out of Place: Silences in Queerness/Raciality*, York: Raw Nerve Books: 9–33.

Hegel, G. W. F. (1807) *The Phenomenology of the Mind*, London: George Allen & Unwin.

Hemmings, C. (2002) *Bisexual Spaces: A Geography of Sexuality and Gender*, London: Routledge.

Hennessy, R. (2000) *Profit and Pleasure: Sexual Identities in Late Capitalism*, London: Routledge.

Hill-Collins, P. (1990) *Black Feminist Thought: Knowledge, Consciousness and the Politics of Empowerment*, London: Verso.

Hines, S. (2005) '"I am a Feminist but…": Transgender Men, Women and Feminism' in J. Reger (ed.) *Different Wavelengths: Studies of the Contemporary Women's Movement*, Routledge: 57–78.

Hines, S. (2006a) 'What's the Difference?: Bringing Particularity to Queer Studies of Transgender', *Journal of Gender Studies*, 15 (1): 49–67.

Hines, S. (2006b) 'Intimate Transitions: Transgender Practices of Partnering and Parenting', *Sociology*, 40 (2): 353–370.

Hines, S. (2006c) 'Social/Cultural Change and Transgender Citizenship', *Sociological Research Online*, 11 (4) http://www.socresonline.org.uk/12/1/hines.html.

Hines, S. (2007a) *TransForming Gender: Transgender Practices of Identity and Intimacy*, Bristol: Policy Press.

Hines, S. (2007b) 'Feminist Theory' in D. Richardson and V. Robinson (eds.) *Introducing Women and Gender Studies* (3rd Ed.), Basingstoke: Palgrave Macmillan.

Hines, S. (2009) 'A Pathway to Diversity?: Human Rights, Citizenship and Politics of Transgender' *Contemporary Politics*, 15 (1): 87–102.

Hines, S. (2010) 'Sexing Gender/Gendering Sex' in Y. Taylor, S. Hines and M. Casey (eds.) *Theorising Intersectionality and Sexuality*, Basingstoke: Palgrave MacMillan: 140–162.

Hines, S and Sanger, T. (eds.) (2010) *Transgender Identities: Towards a Social Analysis of Gender Diversity*, London and New York: Routledge.

Hines, S. and Taylor, Y. (eds.) (2012) *Sexualities: Past Reflections, Future Directions*, Basingstoke: Palgrave Macmillan.

Hird, M. J. (2002) 'For a Sociology of Transsexualism', *Sociology*, 36 (3): 557–595.

Hobson, B. (ed.) (2003) *Recognition Struggles and Social Movements: Contested Identities, Agency and Power*, Cambridge: Cambridge University Press.

Honneth, A. (1995) *The Struggle for Recognition: The Moral Grammar of Social Conflicts*, Cambridge: Polity.

Ingraham, C. (1996) 'The Heterosexual Imaginary: Feminist Sociology and Theories of Gender' in S. Seidman (ed.) *Queer Theory/Sociology*, Cambridge, MA: Blackwell: 168–193.

Jamieson, L. (1998) *Intimacy: Personal Relationships in Modern Society*, Cambridge: Polity Press.

Jay, K. and Young, A. (1992) *Out of the Closets: Voices of Gay Liberation*, New York: New York University Press.

Jeffreys, S. (1997) 'Transgender Activism: A Feminist Perspective' *The Journal of Lesbian Studies*. 1:55–74.

Koyama, E. (2003) 'Transfeminist Manifesto' in R. Dicker and A. Piepmeier (eds.) *Catching a Wave: Reclaiming Feminism for the 21st Century*, Boston, US: Northeastern Press.

Kulpa, R. and Mizielinska, J. (2012) *De-Centering Western Sexualities: Central and Eastern European Perspectives*, Farnham: Ashgate.

Lawler S. (2005) 'Disgusted Subjects: The Making of Middle-class Identities', *The Sociological Review*, 53 (3): 429–446.

Leff, L. (2012) As Gay Pride hits Stride, Transgendered find More Acceptance Associated Press, USATODAY.com, accessed July 2012.

Lewins (1995) *Transsexualism in Society: A Sociology of Male-To-Female Transsexuals*, South Melbourne: Macmillan Education.

Lewis, L. (ed.) (1998) *Forming Nation, Framing Welfare*, London: Routledge.

Lewis, G. (2000) *'"Race", Gender, Social Welfare: Encounters in a Postcolonial Society*, Cambridge: Polity Press.

Lister, R. (1997) *Citizenship: Feminist Perspectives*, Basingstoke and London: Macmillan.

Long, S. (2009) 'Unbearable Witness: How Western Activists (Mis)recognize Sexuality in Iran', *Contemporary Politics*, 5 (15): 119–136.

MacKinnon, C. (1982) 'Feminism, Marxism, Method and the State: An Agenda for Theory', *Signs* 7(3): 515–544.

McDermott, E. (2011) 'The World *Some* Have Won: Sexuality, Class and Inequality', in Y. Taylor (ed.) *Sexualities: Special Issue on Class,* 14 (1): 63–78.

McLaughlin, J., Phillimore, P. and Richardson, D. (eds.) (2011) *Contesting Recognition*, Basingstoke: Palgrave Macmillan.

McNay, L. (2008) *Against Recognition*, Cambridge: Polity.

Merk, M. (2007) 'Sexuality, Subjectivity and... Economics?' in T. Lovell (ed.) *(Mis)recognition, Social Inequality and Social Justice*, London: Routledge.

Mitchell, J. (1973) *Women's Estate*, Harmondsworth: Penguin.

Monro, S. and Warren, T. (2004) 'Transgendering Citizenship', *Sexualities*, 7 (3): 345–362.

Murray Emilio, S. O. (1996) *American Gay*, Chicago: University of Chicago Press.

Nair, I. D. (2009) Against Equality: Queer Challenges to the Politics of Inclusion, http://againstequality.wordpress.com/about/, accessed 20 May 2011.

Nataf, Z. (1996) *Lesbians Talk Transgender*, London: Scarlet Press.

Paine, T. (1792) *Rights of Man: Being an Answer to Mr. Burke's Attack on the French Revolution*, London: J. Johnson.

Pateman, C. (1989) *The Disorder of Women: Disorder, Feminism and Political Theory*, Cambridge: Polity Press.

Phelan, S. (2010) *Sexual Strangers: Gays, Lesbians and Dilemmas of Citizenship*, Philadelphia: Temple University Press.

Phillips, A. (2003) 'Recognition and the Struggle for Political Voice' in B. Hobson (ed.) *Recognition Struggles and Social Movements: Contested Identities, Agency and Power*, Cambridge: Cambridge University Press: 263–273.

Plummer, K. (1995) *Telling Sexual Stories: Power, Change and Social Worlds*, London: Routledge.

Prosser, J. (1998), *Second Skins: The Body Narratives of Transsexuality*, New York: Columbia University Press.

Puar, J. K. (2007) *Terrorist Assemblages: Homonationalism in Queer Times*, Durham: Duke University Press.

Raymond, J. (1980) *The Transsexual Empire*, London: The Women's Press.

Reason and Bradbury (2008) *Handbook of Action Research: Participative Inquiry and Practice, 2nd edition*. London: Sage Publications.
Rich, A. (1980) 'Compulsory Heterosexuality and Lesbian Existence', *Signs*, 5 (4): 631–660.
Richardson, D. (1998) 'Sexuality and Citizenship', *Sociology*, 32: 83–100.
Richardson, D. (2005) 'Desiring Sameness?: The Rise of a Neoliberal Politics of Normalisation', *Antipode*, 37 (3): 515–553.
Richardson, D. and Seidman, S. (eds.) (2002) *Handbook of Lesbian and Gay Studies*, London: Sage.
Richardson, D. and Monro, S. (2012) *Sexuality, Equality and Diversity*, Basingstoke: Palgrave Macmillan.
Riddell, C. (1995) 'Divided Sisterhood: A Critical Review of Janice Raymond's The Transsexual Empire' in R. Ekins and D. King (eds.) *Blending Genders: Social Aspects of Cross-Dressing*, London: Routledge: 171–189.
Rorty, R. (2000) 'Is "Cultural Recognition" a Useful Notion for Leftist Politics?', *Critical Horizons*, 1 (1): 7–20.
Roseneil, S. (2000) 'Queer Frameworks and Queer Tendencies: Towards an Understanding of Postmodern Transformations of Sexuality', *Sociological Research Online*, 5 (3).
Roseneil, S. and Budgeon, S. (2004) 'Beyond the Conventional Family: Intimacy, Care and Community in the 21st Century', *Current Sociology*, 52 (2): 127–134.
Rowbotham, S. (2001) *Promise of a Dream: Remembering the Sixties*, London and New York: Penguin.
Rowbotham, S., Segal, L. and Wainwright, H (1981) *Beyond the Fragments: Feminism and the Making of Socialism*, Boston, US: Alyson Press.
Rubin, G. (1989) 'Thinking Sex: Notes for a Radical Theory of the Politics of Sexuality' in C. Vance (ed.) *Pleasure and Danger: Exploring Female Sexuality*, London: Pandora: 267–319.
Rubin, H. (1996) 'Do You Believe in Gender?' *Sojourner* 21 (6): 7–8.
Sandell, J. (1994) 'The Cultural Necessity of Queer Families', www.popcultures.com/articles/queer.htm. accessed March 2011.
Sandland, R. (2005) 'Feminism and the Gender Recognition Act', *Feminist Legal Studies*, 13 (1): 43–66.
Sanger, T. (2010) *Trans People's Partnerships: Towards an Ethics of Intimacy*, Basingstoke: Palgrave McMillan.
Santos, A. C. (2013) *Social Movements and Sexual Citizenship in Southern Europe*. Basingstoke: Palgrave Macmillan.
Sartre, J. P. (1943) *Being and Nothingness*, trans. H. E. Barnes, London: Routledge.
Savage, M. (2000) *Class Analysis and Social Transformation*, Buckingham: Open University Press.
Schrock, P. and Reid, L. (2006) 'Transsexuals' Sexual Stories', *Archives of Sexual Behaviour*, 35 (1): 75–86.
Scott, J. W. (1992) 'Experience' in J. Butler and J. W. Scott (eds.) *Feminists Theorize the Political*, New York: Routledge: 22–40.

Sedgwick, E. (1993) *Tendencies*, Durham, NC: Duke University Press.

Segal, L. (2007) *Making Trouble: Life and Politics*, London: Serpents Tail.

Seidman, S. (1997) *Difference Troubles: Queering Social Theory and Sexual Politics*, Cambridge: Cambridge University Press.

Skeggs, B. (1997) *Formations of Class and Gender: Becoming Respectable*, London: Sage.

Skeggs, B. (2011) 'Imagining Personhood Differently: person Value and Autonomist Working-Class Value Practices', *The Sociological Review*, 59 (3): 579–594.

Stacey, J. (1996) *In the Name of the Family: Rethinking Family Values in the Postmodern Age*, Boston: Beacon Press.

Stone, S. (1991) 'The Empire Strikes Back: A Posttranssexual Manifesto' in J. Epstein and K. Straub (eds.) *Body Guards: The Cultural Politics of Gender Ambiguity*, London and N.Y: Routledge: 280-304.

Stonewall (2005) *A Guide to Civil Partnerships*, www.stonewallcymru.org.uk/ other/ accessed February 2013.

Stryker, S. www.comptonscafeteriariot.orgaccessed June 2012.

Stryker, S. and Whittle, S. (eds.) (1996) *The Transgender Studies Reader*, New York and Abingdon: Routledge.

Stychin, C. (1998) *A Nation by Rights: National Cultures, Sexual Identity Politics, and the Discourse of Human Rights*, Philadelphia: Temple University Press.

Sullivan, A. (1995) *Virtually Normal: An Argument about Homosexuality*. New York: Knopf.

Tatchell, P. (2005) 'Civil Partnerships are Sexual Apartheid', http://www.petertatchell.net/lgbt_rights/partnerships/sexualapartheid.htm, accessed March 2012.

Taylor, C. (1995) *Philosophical Arguments*, Cambridge, MA: Harvard University Press.

Taylor, Y. (2007) *Working-class Lesbian Life Experiences: Classed Outsiders*, Basingstoke: Palgrave Macmillan.

Taylor. Y. (2008) 'Un/Civil Partnerships: Class in Lesbian Relationships' in M.L. Kohlke and L. Orza (eds.) *Critical Issues Series Persons and Sexuality*, 44: www.inter-disciplinary.net/publishing/idp/eBooks/.

Taylor, Y. (2009) *Lesbian and Gay Parenting: Securing Social and Educational Capital*, Basingstoke: Palgrave Macmillan.

Taylor, Y. (2012) *Fitting into Place? Class and Gender Geographies and Temporalities*, Farnham: Ashgate.

Taylor, Y., Hines, S. and Casey, M. (eds.) (2011) *Theorising Intersexuality and Sexuality*, Basingstoke: Palgrave Macmillan.

Thompson, S. (2006) *The Political Theory of Recognition: A Critical Introduction*, Cambridge: Polity.

Tully, B. (1992) *Accounting for Transsexualism and Transhomosexuality*, London: Whiting and Birch.

Turner, B.S. and Hamilton, P. (1994) *Citizenship. Critical Concepts*, London: Routledge.

Waite, M. (2009) 'Critique of "Sexual Orientation" and "Gender Identity"' in Human Rights Discourse: Global Queer Politics Beyond the Yogyakarta Principles, *Contemporary Politics*, 15 (1):137–156.
Walby, S. (1994)) 'Is Citizenship Gendered?', *Sociology*, 28 (2): 107–121.
Warner, M. (1993) (ed.) *Fear of a Queer Planet*, Minneapolis, MN: University of Minnesota Press.
Watney, S. (1994) *Practices of Freedom: Selected Writings on HIV/AIDS*, London: Rivers Oram Press.
Weeks, J. (2000) *Making Sexual History*, Cambridge: Polity Press.
Weeks, J. (2007) *The World We Have Won: The Making of Erotic and Intimate Life*, London: Routledge.
Weeks, J., Heaphy, B. and Donovan, C. (2004) *Same Sex Intimacies: Families of Choice and Other Life Experiments*, London and New York: Routledge.
Weston, K. (1991) *Families We Choose: Lesbians, Gays, Kinship*, New York: Columbia University Press
Whittle, S. (2002) 'Goodwin & I v. United Kingdom Government: What Does It Mean? Analysis of the Implications of the ECtHR Judgments in the Cases of *Goodwin v. UK* and *I v UK' Press for Change@* http://www.pfc.org.uk/node/352 (accessed March 2008).
Wilchins, (1997) *Read My Lips: Sexual Subversion and the End of Gender*, Ann Arbor, MI: Firebrand Books.
Wilkinson, E. (2009) 'The Emotions Least Relevant to Politics? Queering Autonomous Activism', *Emotion, Space and Society*, 2 (1): 36–43.
Wilkinson, E. (2012) 'The Romantic Imaginary: Compulsory Coupledom and Single Existence' in S. Hines, and Y. Taylor, (eds.) (2012) *Sexualities: Past Reflections, Future Directions*, Basingstoke: Palgrave Macmillan.
Wilson, E. (1982) *Mirror Writing: An Autobiography*, London: Pandora.
Young, I. M. (1989) 'Polity and Group Difference: A Critique of the Idea of Universal Citizenship', *Ethics*, 99 (2): 250–274.
Young, I. M. (1990) *Justice and the Politics of Difference*, Princeton: Princeton University Press.
Young, I. M. (1997) *Intersecting Voices: Dilemmas of Gender, Political Philosophy, and Policy*, Princeton: Princeton University Press.
Young, I. M. (2000) *Inclusion and Democracy*, Oxford: Oxford University Press.
Young, I. M. (2008) 'Unruly Categories: A Critique of Nancy Fraser's Dual Systems Theory' in K. Olson (ed.) *Adding Insult to Injury: Nancy Fraser Debates Her Critics*, London: Verso: 147–160.

Index

Printed and bound in Great Britain by
CPI Group (UK) Ltd, Croydon, CR0 4YY